AN INTRODUCTION TO HAIKU

HAROLD G. HENDERSON was born in New York City in 1889 and took his B.A., M.A., and a degree in Chemical Engineering from Columbia University. From 1927–29 he was assistant to the curator of Far Eastern Art at the Metropolitan Museum of Art. In 1930 he went to Japan, where he lived the following three years. On his return to this country he joined the faculty at Columbia University, where he taught Japanese and initiated a course in the history of Japanese art. He retired in 1955. His publications include The Bamboo Broom (1933), The Surviving Works of Sharaku (with Louis V. Ledoux) (1939), A Handbook of Japanese Grammar (1942). He has also translated H. Minamato's "Illustrated History of Japanese Art" (1934), etc. In 1960 he was decorated by the Japanese government with the Order of the Sacred Treasure.

AN INTRODUCTION TO
HAIKU

AN ANTHOLOGY OF POEMS AND POETS
FROM BASHŌ TO SHIKI

Harold G. Henderson

DOUBLEDAY ANCHOR BOOKS
DOUBLEDAY & COMPANY, INC.
GARDEN CITY, NEW YORK

To M. B. H.

Anchor Books edition: 1958

COVER PAINTING BY GEN INOKUMA

COVER DESIGN BY REMY CHARLIP

TYPOGRAPHY BY EDWARD GOREY

CONTENTS

Preface

THIS book is an outgrowth from a small book on haiku, called *The Bamboo Broom*, which was published just twenty-five years ago and which is now out of print. It contains about seventy-five translations which originally appeared in the *Broom*, and some three hundred new ones.

In the preface to the *Broom* I referred to the old Italian adage *"traduttore, traditore,"* and its implication that any translator is probably a traitor. For the present book it is even more necessary to emphasize the warning, because the very number of examples may suggest that they include all kinds of haiku, which they do not. An ideal translation should, I believe, reproduce the effect of the original, but I have found that the best any translator can even hope for is to reproduce the effect that the originals have had on him. And there are many famous poems, in English as well as in Japanese, that are undoubtedly fine, but from which I can get no effect at all. Furthermore, there are many haiku, particularly those with very delicate suggestions—and the strength of haiku lies in its suggestions—for which I can find no even passable English equivalents. The sampling of haiku given here is therefore necessarily a partial one.

The principle of this sampling, at least as far as the most important poets are concerned, has been to take for discussion their most famous poems, and such others as seemed necessary to illustrate their characters and their art. Those that follow the text are haiku which I believe can stand alone in their present English translations, and give at least some of the effect of the originals even to those readers who have made no special study of Japan. This method is a compromise, and not wholly satisfactory. Bashō, for example, wrote some eight hundred poems that can be dated to his great period, the last ten years of his life; of these, I have here translated only sixty. But I have no more translations that I think can stand alone, and I have a very strong belief that too much explanation can take the pleasure out of any poetry.

My intention has been to write English verse which will be faithful to the spirit of the originals, and will at the same time approximate literal translation, but there are certain peculiarities about Japanese which make absolute literalness practically impossible. First, there are no articles in the Japanese language, practically no pronouns, and in general no distinctions between singular and plural. I have therefore felt at liberty to supply these, as well as omitted prepositions,* though the original haiku gain in effect from their very compactness.

Second, there is no punctuation in haiku, its place being taken by *kireji* (literally "cut-words") such as *ya, kana, keri,* and the like, which have no translatable meaning, but which often indicate an unfinished sentence, and which have in addition an elusive force of their own. I have therefore tried to give the effect

---

* Japanese "prepositions" come after the word they modify and therefore are really "postpositions." Cf. the appendix.

of these *kireji* by the use of punctuation marks and interjections, and occasionally by finishing sentences with simple verbs like "is" or "was" or "do."

Third, the Japanese language is constructed differently from ours; there are, for example, no relative pronouns—any descriptive clause must precede its noun—and I was often confronted with the dilemma of whether to try to follow the strict grammatical form or whether to follow the order of thought. In most of my translations I have chosen to follow the order of thought, and to supply the comparatively unimportant intermediate words in accordance with English standards. I have also, once in a great while, supplied more important words which are implied but not expressed in the original.

To each of my translations I have appended a footnote giving the original Japanese, and as accurate English equivalents for the Japanese words as possible. By consulting these footnotes the reader may be able to appreciate the terseness that is one of the joys of the original, and make his contact with the poet more direct. The English "equivalents" cannot, of course, be more than a guide. There are very few Japanese words that have one, and only one, English equivalent, and the particles (*kireji*, "postpositions," etc.) often have none at all. (The effect of these particles is discussed at some length in the appendix.) Readers who do not know Japanese should remember that any qualifying clause must precede its noun, and that any normal sentence ends in a verb. This tends to make the Japanese order of thought often the exact opposite of ours. Thus, for example, a phrase like "*sama-zama no mono omoidasu sakura*," which in the Japanese order is literally "many-kinds-of things bring-to-mind cherry-bloom," would be grammatically equivalent to "cherry blossoms which bring to mind things of many kinds."

For those who may care to read the originals, I should state that in the transliterations consonants are pronounced as in English, except that the "g" is always hard, and a doubled consonant is always pronounced twice, as in "cattail," not just once as in "cattle." Vowels are pronounced as in Italian, and are short unless marked "long"; vowels marked "long" (like "ō") are really combinations of two short vowels, and in Japanese are written as such (e.g. ō = ŏŏ). There are no diphthongs; "haiku," for example, is a three syllable word: "ha-i-ku." If anyone wishes to do "syllable-counting" he should remember that Japanese count in "*ji-on*," which correspond only roughly to English syllables. Most *ji-on* are either vowels or short syllables ending in a vowel; but the "n" that in English would conclude a syllable (as in "ban") is also a *ji-on,* as is the first of any doubled consonant. E.g. "teppatsu" (te-p-pa-tsu) and "Onjō (O-n-jo-o) both have four *ji-on.*

It will be noticed that there is no rhyme in the originals, and my use of it in the English rendering of haiku therefore needs defense. First, I happen to like rhyme in a short poem of this sort, and I think that it is at least allowable. The chief reason that the Japanese do not use it is that all Japanese words end either in a vowel or in "n," and rhyming would soon become intolerably monotonous. Secondly, I think that any verse form, be it sonnet, triolet, or haiku, is more effective if it is kept fairly rigid, so that it can act as a sort of frame to the picture. In Japanese the effect of definite form is given by an alteration of five and seven syllables; in English this method is impossible, and the use of rhyme or assonance, especially if it can be kept unobtrusive, is perhaps the best available substitute. Thirdly, haiku are very short, and their grammar is often fragmentary. There is real danger that a literal translation might be mistaken for an unfinished piece of prose, and a haiku is not that, but a poem, complete as it stands.

If the reading and writing of English haiku ever becomes general, some better form than the one used in this book can doubtless be found. I can only hope that the readers of this book will join in the search for it.

Before closing this preface I ought to make it clear that all titles to haiku are my own invention, as there are no titles to the originals. Many haiku, however, occur in works that are primarily prose, like Bashō's diaries; others are preceded by forewords of varying length which explain the circumstances that inspired them. When haiku such as these are given out of context, titles become almost a necessity; they are put with other haiku mainly for the sake of uniformity, and are, I hope, usually innocuous.

I must also give my thanks to Mr. Ryusaku Tsunoda, my colleague at Columbia for some twenty years, whose wide knowledge and wise counsel has been of inestimable value; to Mr. R. H. Blyth, with whom my personal contacts have been most stimulating even outside the haiku world, and in whose monumental four-volume work on haiku (published by Hokusaidō, Tokyo) I have found a number of poems that I had not come across elsewhere; and most of all to my wife, whose name really ought to be on the title page.

Chapter I

CHARACTERISTICS
OF HAIKU

THERE are several arts which are so widely practiced in Japan that they may be considered an integral part of its culture but which are nevertheless practically unknown to the world at large. Among these are the twin arts of reading and of writing haiku. These two are ancient arts—ancient, at least, as we in America count age—for their seeds were sown well over seven hundred years ago, and it was in the seventeenth century that they blossomed into full perfection. But they are modern arts as well, more widespread today than they ever were before. Just how many Japanese do practice them no one knows exactly, for most haiku are composed primarily for the pleasure of the author and his friends and not for publication. We do know, however, that hundreds of thousands of new haiku are published every year.*

* In 1957 there were about fifty monthly magazines devoted to haiku, most of them successful commercial ventures. The issues that I have been able to check contain a minimum of fifteen hundred haiku each. Many haiku ap-

The language barrier prevents most foreigners from doing the reading and the writing of haiku in the original Japanese. Fortunately, however, there are many haiku, much of whose effect can be kept in accurate translation. And there is no reason why haiku should not be written in English or any other language.

Perhaps it would be as well to try to explain just what a haiku is; but this is not so easy as it seems, for probably no two Japanese would quite agree on exactly what constitutes a haiku. Primarily it is a poem; and being a poem it is intended to express and to evoke emotion. It is necessary to insist upon this point, because it has been the custom in the past to translate "haiku" into "epigram," and this is quite misleading. Secondly, a haiku is a very short poem, with a traditional and classic form, and with special characteristics of its own.

Sir Arthur Quiller-Couch has pointed out that the capital difficulty of verse consists "in saying ordinary unemotional things, of bridging the flat intervals between high moments." Now, by its very shortness a haiku avoids this difficulty almost automatically. Haiku may be of many kinds, grave or gay, deep or shallow, religious, satirical, sad, humorous, or charming; but all haiku worthy of the name are records of high moments—higher, at least, than the surrounding plain. And in the hands of a master a haiku can be the concentrated essence of pure poetry.

Because the haiku is shorter than other forms of

---

pear also in other publications—even in the counterpart of our *Wall Street Journal*. I believe the total is probably well over a million.

There are also about fifty magazines devoted to the other popular verse form, the *tanka* (described in Chapter II). The actual number of *tanka* published yearly seems to be about half that of haiku.

poetry it naturally has to depend for its effect on the power of suggestion, even more than they do. As haiku are studied further, it will be seen that they usually gain their effect not only by suggesting a mood, but also by giving a clear-cut picture which serves as a starting point for trains of thought and emotion. But, again owing to their shortness, haiku can seldom give the picture in detail. Only the outlines or important parts are drawn, and the rest the reader must fill in for himself. Haiku indeed have a very close resemblance to the "ink sketches" so dear to the hearts of the Japanese.

Perhaps it would be simplest to give an example taken from modern English poetry. The climax of Edward Shanks' lovely *A Night Piece*, for instance, in its spirit is pure haiku of the highest order:

> So far . . . so low . . .
> A drowsy thrush? A waking nightingale?
> Silence. We do not know.

The rest of the poem is spent in filling in the details of the picture and in preparing us for this high moment. It is fine in itself, but by haiku standards quite unneeded. These lines alone show us that the time *must* be at dusk, the season *must* be spring or early summer, and the scene *must* be some secluded place where there is only silence or a half-heard song.

There are twenty-four lines in the original poem. A haiku lover could get their cumulative effect by repeating the haiku part of the poem ten or a dozen times. Indeed, the only point on which these lines might fail to pass the most meticulous tests for haiku is that the last sentence is subjective, and unnecessary except in so far as it shows that the listener has with him a companion with whom he is in sympathy.

It is interesting to compare these lines with a very famous haiku by the great master Bashō:

A cloud of blossoms,
an evening bell—
Ueno? Asakusa?

The season here is spring, with cherry blossoms everywhere, for "blossoms" in haiku are cherry blossoms always; and a Japanese would know that the time is evening, even though the original says simply "bell," for the only bells that could be heard were temple bells—Kaneiji at Ueno, Sensōji at Asakusa—and these it was the custom to sound at dusk. The scene, of course, is some spot in Tokyo from which the thickset blossoms at both places can be seen, and the bells at least half heard. (The poem was actually written in Bashō's hut on the banks of the Sumida River, a mile or so below Asakusa.) The surface sense of quiet, and the underlying feeling of a mystery that is essentially religious, are much the same as in *A Night Piece*. But here they are given with an even surer touch, for Bashō was a past master in not "putting words between the truth and ourselves."

These examples perhaps will show why haiku reading is in itself an art, and why in order really to understand a good haiku one has to read it over many times. It is not that the picture is hazy in any way, for if the author has done his work properly, the picture is quite clear. The point is that good haiku are full of overtones. The elusiveness that is one of their chief charms comes, not from haziness, but from the fact that so much suggestion is put into so few words.

Hana-no-kumo | *kane* | *wa* | *Ueno* | *ka* | *Asakusa* | *ka*
Blossom-cloud | [temple] bell | as-for | Ueno | ? | Asakusa | ?

In order to produce their effect, haiku writers make great use of what they call *rensō* or association of ideas, and this they do in several different ways. The older haiku-makers came to the conclusion that one experience common to all men was the change of weather with the different seasons, and so introduced into nearly all their poems what is known as a *ki*, or "season." This means that in nearly all their haiku there is some word or expression that indicates the time of year, and so forms a background for the picture that they are trying to bring up in the reader's mind. Such a *kigo* (season word) may be a definite naming of the season, like "summer heat" or "autumn wind," or a mere suggestion, like a reference to plum blossoms or to snow. The custom of using *kigo* has hardened into an almost inviolable rule, and most modern collections of haiku arrange their contents according to the seasons to which the poems refer.

It may be noted in passing that the use of *ki* is probably at the base of a charge that has been advanced that haiku are more concerned with nature than with human affairs. Such a statement is ridiculous. Haiku are more concerned with human emotions than with human acts, and natural phenomena are used to reflect human emotions, but that is all. The older and simpler forerunners of haiku may make the comparison in definite words, as in this, by Moritake (1452–1549):

> A morning-glory!
> And so—today!—may seem
> my own life-story.

Asagao | ni | kyō | wa | miyuran | waga | yo | kana
Morning-glory | as | today | as-for | may-appear | my | life | *kana*

meaning, of course, "I too may die today; and if I do . . ." But this was written before the haiku form had come into its own, and later poets preferred to get their effects by somewhat more subtle suggestion.

There are many other things suggested by *ki*, and just as morning-glories bring up thoughts of quickly fading beauty, so do the autumn winds suggest sadness, and plum blossoms the promise of perfect beauty to be attained by the later cherry blooms. It should be mentioned that the word "cuckoo" has not the same associations as with us. The song of the *hototogisu*, the little Japanese cuckoo, is usually heard at dusk. It is considered to be not only beautiful, but also slightly sad; other names for the *hototogisu* are "bird of the other world," "bird of disappointed love," etc.

As would naturally be expected, many haiku evoke associations by references to Buddhist beliefs, to social customs, and to episodes in Japanese history that every Japanese would know. Unfortunately these references would be as unintelligible to the Western reader as the connotations of Easter, Thanksgiving, or Guy Fawkes' Day would be to the average Japanese, and therefore haiku containing them call for so much explanation that they have had to be inadequately represented here.

Besides these, there is another form of association of ideas to which special attention must be drawn, as it is used in many haiku. This is a comparison of two or more ideas expressed in the poem itself, and it must always be looked for. In some haiku the comparison is obvious, as in this one, which is by the modern poet Kwaso:

The tower high
I climb; there, on that fir top,
sits a butterfly!

Here the point is in the contrast, while in Sodō's trinity of early summer:

Green leaves to see,
a mountain cuckoo, and the first
bonito—all three!

the point is the piling up of the similar effects of three delightful things acting simultaneously on three different senses. (To a Japanese the first bonito is as much a delicacy as the first trout is to us.)

These two examples are quite simple and without any very deep meaning, but in other haiku the comparison of ideas may be so hidden that the author's intention will be realized only after repeated readings. It is interesting, though not important here, to note that the use of this particular form of association is probably due to the influence of Chinese classics, just as a Latin influence can be found in the inversions to which we are accustomed in our own poetry.

There is still another device which haiku-makers use to condense the expression of their thoughts. That is the omission of words which would be required in a grammatically formed sentence but which are not really needed to make the sense clear. It is a device which is extremely effective when used with discretion, but when second-rate writers use it to excess

To | ni | noreba | sugi-no | kozue | ni | chō | hitotsu
Tower | on | when-I-climb | cryptomeria's | top-twig | on | butterfly | one

Me | ni | aoba | yama-hototogisu | hatsu | katsuo
Eyes | in | green-leaves | mountain-cuckoo | first | bonito

it may result in haiku that are more like puzzles than poems. The effect of haziness produced by over-condensation, however, should never be confused with the difficulty of understanding some of the great haiku, which may not give out their full meaning, even to those who are trained in the art of reading, until an explanation is given of the circumstances under which they were written. Really great haiku suggests so much that more words would lessen their meaning.

In addition to such general characteristics as have been discussed above, there are certain technical conventions which would have to be known to anyone who wishes to go back to the originals. Most important are the uses of the *kireji*, or "cut-words," like *kana*, which usually marks the end of a haiku, and *ya*, which divides a haiku into two parts that are to be equated or compared. (These are further discussed in the appendix.) Other conventions have grown up around the uses of *kigo*, the "season words." (In the absence of any other indication, a reference to deer means that the time is autumn, etc., etc.) I have not discussed them, because I have felt that where the season was not obvious it could be indicated in a title or a footnote. Nearly all such conventions are used primarily to eliminate unnecessary words. According to Japanese standards, most of my translations are much too long. But I hope they are short enough to enable the reader to follow the advice given me by my first instructor in haiku. That was to read through a number of haiku each evening until I found one that suited my mood; to learn it by heart; and then to go to bed with it.

Chapter II

EARLY HAIKU

THE origin of haiku—or at least the origin of the seventeen-syllable form of verse—is lost in the dimness of antiquity. We know that from very early times the Japanese used alternate lines of five and seven syllables as a poetic rhythm. We also know that one very popular early verse form was the *tanka*, a poem of thirty-one syllables arranged 5, 7, 5, 7, 7, and that one of the Court amusements used to be "verse-capping," in which the first three lines of a *tanka* would be given, the competitors being required to supply the remaining two. These first three lines were in the haiku form, and it is certain that we have here the seeds of haiku, but we have no record of the first production of poems that were complete in seventeen syllables.*

* Haiku were originally called "hokku," literally "starting verse." At present the names "haiku" and "hokku" are used almost interchangeably. Hokku are still used as the starting verses of *renga* (linked verses; i.e., poems continued by several authors alternately), but these cannot be considered here. The best book on the subject in English is *Minase Sangin Hyakuin*, by Kenneth Yasuda, Kogakusha Co., Ltd., Tokyo, 1956.

The earliest extant poems of haiku form date from the beginning of the thirteenth century, and it is indicative of their close relationship with *tanka* that one of the best known of these is by Fujiwara no Sadaiye, reputed to be the compiler of the famous *tanka* anthology, *Hyakunin Isshu* (about A.D. 1235). It is, however, a disputed question whether any of these early attempts is worthy of the name "haiku." Personally, I am inclined to think that some of them are. Sadaiye's

> A fluttering swarm
> of cherry petals—and there comes,
> pursuing them, the storm!

is not fully developed haiku, but at least it gives a picture and a mood, and the author's feeling about life as he saw it. The fact that he was probably thinking of the maids of honor at the Imperial Court does not detract from the poetry.

Other early seventeen-syllable verses have also been preserved, many of them being by high officials and military leaders. The form, however, did not become really popular until some two hundred and fifty years later, about the beginning of the sixteenth century. At that time, the two most prominent poets were Moritake (1452–1540) and Sōkan (1465–1553). Both wrote verses that are still remembered, but they are of very different kinds.

Moritake was a Shinto priest of high rank, and much of his best work was inspired by religion. The poem already quoted (page 5) is almost a sermon. Even his most famous poem:

Chiru | *hana* | *wo* | *oikakete* | *yuku* | *arashi* | *kana*
Fall-scattering | blossoms | [acc.] | pursuing | go | storm | *kana*

> Fallen petals rise
>> back to the branch—I watch:
>>> oh . . . butterflies!

is inspired by a line of scripture that asks: "Can a fallen blossom return to its branch?"

Sōkan's verses are apt to be clever conceits like:

> If to the moon
>> one puts a handle—what
>>> a splendid fan!

This sort of thing is hardly real haiku—or real poetry—even though it does suggest the perfect fullness of the moon, the pleasure of looking at it so that it seems attached to a tree branch, and the cool of a summer night after a hot day. The reason that it is "not haiku" is that it is not even meant to express or to evoke any real emotion.

The next hundred years cover the ending of the Ashikaga regime, with its accompanying civil wars; the temporary headship of Hideyoshi; and the establishment of a new "military" government, the Tokugawa Shogunate. The times did not favor delicate poetry, and haiku went from bad to worse, the making of seventeen-syllable verses finally becoming little more than a parlor game in which the authors spent their time on tortured ingenuities. For instance, the foremost poet of the early Tokugawa days, Teitoku (d. 1653), wishing to celebrate a New Year's Day

Rak-ka | eda | ni | kaeru | to | mireba | kochō | kana
Fallen-blossoms | branch | to | return | that | when-see | butterflies | *kana*

Tsuki | ni | e | wo | sashitarabs | yoki | uchiwa | kana
Moon | to | handle | [acc.] | if-attach | good | round-fan | *kana*

which happened to be the beginning of the "cow" *
year, wrote as follows:

> This morning, how
> icicles drip!—Slobbering
> year of the cow!

This is cleverer than it sounds in translation, for
"*taruru tsurara*" is onomatopoeic, and "*taruru*" also has
the meaning of "hang down." But it is trick work,
emphatically "not haiku," and one can understand why
even the gentle Bashō referred to verses of this sort
as "Teitoku's slobber."

It would be wrong to give the impression that all
contemporary haiku were quite as unpoetic as this.
Even Teitoku often had really poetic ideas, though he
usually seems to be more concerned with the joke than
with the poetry in his haiku. Quite typical of his better
work is his verse in praise of the *utsugi* (the shrub,
Deutzia scabra):

> It lets one see
> snow, moon, and blossoms—all at once.
> Oh, *utsugi!*

the point here being that "snow, moon, and flowers"
(*setsu-gek-ka*) is a traditional trinity of beauty, and
that the little white flowers on the *utsugi* bushes, when

* Years used to be counted in a series of twelve, named
for the rat, ox, tiger, hare, dragon, snake, horse, sheep,
monkey, bird, dog, and boar. Ushi { means } ox, bull, or cow.
                                    { is }

Kesa | *taruru* | *tsurara* | *ya* | *yodare-no* | *ushi-no* | *toshi*
This-morning | drip | icicles | ya | slobbering | cow's |
year

Setsugekka | *ichi-dō-ni* | *miyuru* | *utsugi* | *kana*
Snow-moon-flowers | at-one-time | can-be-seen | deutzia |
kana

seen in moonlight, do look a bit like snow. "*Utsugi* in moonlight" is also in itself a traditional symbol for beauty. All this is pleasant as well as ingenious, but not great poetry by any standard.

However, better times were in sight. The peace, and perhaps to some extent also the repression that the new military government imposed, seems to have encouraged the haiku mood. Even Teitoku's pupils were better poets than he was, and many of their poems show a great sensitiveness to natural beauty.

Teishitsu, for example, when he went to see the celebrated cherry blooms of Yoshino, on his return was asked what haiku he had composed; and his answer is often called the most perfect tribute possible:

> "Oh . . . . . !"
> That's all—upon the blossom-covered
> hills of Yoshino!

This, in the original at least, is undoubtedly genuine poetry. Nevertheless there is still a certain thinness about these productions, and it is not until we come to Sōin, the founder of the Danrin School (c. 1660), that we get an insight into what haiku were destined to be. In spite of the pseudo-cynicism of the attitude, a poem like Sōin's:

> Dewdrops, limpid, small—
> and such a lack of judgment shown
> in where they fall!

Kore | wa | kore | wa | to | bakari | hana-no | Yoshinoyama
"This | as-for | this | as-for" | thus | only | blossom's | Yoshino hills

Shiratsuyu | ya | mufunbetsunaru | okidokoro
White-dews | ya | undiscriminated | settling-places

is already in a different world from Teitoku.

It is worth while stopping for a moment to consider this difference. In the earlier poems the author's complete meaning could be put into words. Here it is impossible to do so. Even Teishitsu is not saying much more than: "When I climb the hills of Yoshino in cherry-blossom time, their beauty leaves me speechless. Much has been said and written of it, but there are in the world beauties for which no speech is adequate, and this is one of them." But when one comes to Sōin's poem—which of course is not only a picture of dews falling on all sorts of places, but which also brings up thoughts of our short human life—and tries to put all its connotations into words, one finds that it cannot be done: this is haiku.

It is true that Sōin was unable to get completely away from puns and other tricks, so that today the Danrin School are the "dunces" of haiku. But Bashō himself called Sōin "the leader of the party of improvement" (*chūkōtōzan*), and said that had it not been for Sōin the people of his own time "would still be licking up Teitoku's slobber."

Chapter III

MATSUO BASHŌ

SHORTLY after 1600 the chaos of civil war that had prevailed for centuries was brought to an end, and Tokugawa Ieyasu established the Shogunate, a military government that allowed no rivals and was only nominally subordinate to the Emperor. In 1638, under the third shogun, a completely pacified Japan was officially isolated from the world, and in 1644 Matsuo Bashō was born.

Bashō would probably have been a poet in any age, but that in which he found himself was peculiarly favorable for the development and appreciation of his genius. Life for all was once more stable and secure; a rich and leisured *bourgeoisie* was being born; and samurai—men of the warrior class—who could no longer turn their energies to the arts of war, tended to turn them to the arts of peace. And of these arts poetry was one of the most popular.

At the age of eight—possibly later, accounts differ—Bashō, who was of samurai blood, was taken into the service of a nobleman, the lord of a castle in Iga, in

the south of Japan. There he became the page of the
lord's son, Sengin, a lad just a few years older than
Bashō himself. The two lived in close companionship,
with Sengin not so much Bashō's master as his close
friend and guide. From Sengin, and from Sengin's master, Kigin, Bashō learned the art of poetry as it was
then known.

Apparently Bashō started composing at the age of
nine, but his first recorded verse—it is hardly a poem
by any standards—dates from the time he was about
thirteen. It was written for the year of the bird (1657),
and is a sort of *jeu d'esprit* rejoicing that that year
falls between the years of the dog and the monkey,
which it does in the Japanese table of calendar signs.

> Oh! It's the friend
>   of the dog and the monkey!
>   The year of the bird!

In its way this effort is almost a caricature of contemporary verse, as it depends for its effect on a "literary"
allusion. Only in this case the allusion is to a story
any Japanese child would know—the tale of Momotarō,
a boy who slew many demons with the help of his
three retainers, a dog, a pheasant, and a monkey.

In 1666 Lord Sengin suddenly died, and within two
months Bashō had gone to the monastery at Kōyasan
and had "renounced the world." There can be no
doubt that he was utterly broken up at the death of his
much-loved master, and that the impression it made
influenced his entire life. More than twenty years later
he went back to Iga in the spring, and stood again

Inu | *to* | *saru-no* | *nakadachi* | *nare* | *-ya* | *tori-no* | *toshi*
Dog | and | monkey's | companion | being | -ya | bird's |
year

Nare-ya has a sort of suggestion of "Is that why it is?"

under the cherry trees where he and Sengin had
worked and played so long, and with a heart too full
to make a normal poem, all he could say was:

> Many, many things
>   they bring to mind—
>   cherry blossoms!

However, though Bashō had given up "the world,"
this did not mean that he confined himself to a monastery, and we next hear of him at Kyoto, studying
haiku under Kigin and beginning to make a name for
himself. When Kigin went to Edo (the present
Tokyo), Bashō followed him; and two years later,
when he was thirty, Bashō started a school of his own,
taking as his first pupil the son of a rich merchant, a
young boy who afterward became famous in his own
right under the name of Kikaku.

Bashō had not at this time reached the height of
his powers, but there is a famous tale of the period
that well illustrates his attitude toward poetry. One
day when he and Kikaku were going through the
fields, looking at the darting dragonflies, the boy made
a seventeen-syllable verse:

> "Red dragonflies!
>   Take off their wings,
>   and they are pepper pods!"

"No!" said Bashō, "that is not haiku. If you wish to
make a haiku on the subject, you must say:

Sama | *-zama-no* | *mono* | *omoidasu* | *sakura* | *kana*
Many | -many | things | bring to mind | cherries | *kana*

Cherry blossoms are particularly associated with samurai
who die young. In the collected poems this is headed
simply *Memories of the Past*.

"Red pepper pods!
Add wings to them,
    and they are dragonflies!"

Gradually Bashō's school increased in numbers and repute, and in the next few years in addition to his haiku he contributed to several books of *renga* or "linked verses." In 1679 he wrote his first verse in the "new style," which came to be associated with his name and was taken as a model by many later haiku poets. This verse, even more important for its technique than its contents, was:

On a withered branch
a crow has settled—
    autumn nightfall.

There are at least two points of technique which made it a model. First, the over-all mood or emotion is produced by a simple description, a plain statement of fact which makes a picture. Second, the two parts that make up the whole are compared to each other, not in simile or metaphor, but as two phenomena, each of which exists in its own right. This may be called "the principle of internal comparison" in which the differences are just as important as the likenesses. Here it is not simply that "over the withered landscape the autumn nightfall settles like a crow." It is also the contrast of the small black body of the crow with the vast amorphous darkness of the nightfall—and what-

Kare-eda | *ni* | *karasu-no* | *tomari-keri* | *aki-no-kure*
Withered-branch | on | crow's | settling-*keri* |
autumn-nightfall

In an earlier version *-taru ya* is used in place of *-keri*. The use of *ya* emphasizes the comparison, and so tends to detract from the unity of the picture as a whole.

ever else the reader may find in it. It is easy to see how the use of this technique helps to give depth to haiku, and to make them starting points for thought and imagination.

Bashō himself did not always follow this model, but in most of his subsequent haiku—even those that are not so wholly objective—"internal comparison" is at least implied. Unless this is realized, much of the effect of his poems is lost. A good illustration is the haiku given on page 17 where the cherry blossoms (emblems of transient beauty) are used both as background and for comparison with what they "bring to mind."

At the time the "crow" verse was written Bashō was consciously looking for the poetic beauty to be found in things not themselves particularly beautiful. He was still developing both his technique and his poetic insight. Two years later, in 1681, something happened to him. He announced that his life, simple as it was, was "too worldly," and he began the serious study of Zen—the Buddhist sect which gives most attention to contemplation. It was after this, in the last ten years of his life, that nearly all of his finest poetry was written.

Early in 1686 Bashō wrote what is probably the best-known haiku in the Japanese language—one which he himself considered as marking the most important turning point in his poetic life. The poem itself is deceptively simple. Literally translated, it is:

> Old pond:
>   frog jump-in
>   water-sound.

Furu-ike | ya | kawazu | tobi-komu | mizu-no-oto
Old-pond | : | frog | jump-in | water-sound

Many competent critics have found in this a deep and esoteric meaning; others have considered it too darkly mysterious to understand at all. Perhaps some light may be thrown by the fact that the last two lines were the first to be composed. The circumstances seem well attested. Bashō was sitting in the garden of his little house in Edo with some of his friends and pupils, when suddenly a sound was heard, necessarily during a period of silence. Bashō, without premeditation, looked up and said: *"Kawazu tobikomu mizu no oto"* (frog-jump-in water-sound). This was immediately recognized as a possible ending for a haiku, and after the others had made various suggestions, Bashō completed it with "old pond" for the first line. If this story is correct, the closest possible English for the poem would seem to be:

> Old pond—
> and a frog-jump-in
> water-sound.

In form this is quite similar to the "crow" poem, but the "internal comparison" between the old pond and the sudden sound is certainly deeper and much more subtle than that between the crow and the autumn nightfall. And the over-all mood induced by it certainly reflects a very different attitude toward life.

If this were the only poem that Bashō had ever written, one might wonder whether the poet really put into it all the deep meaning that one finds. But the proof is overwhelming that, consciously or unconsciously, Bashō did put into most if not all of his later haiku all the meaning that anyone can find, and probably much more. It has been my own experience that the more one reads them, the more one finds depths in each single one, even in those that appear most trivial. One gets a feeling that they are somehow all

parts of one whole. Japanese who have had the same
experience have explained it by saying that Bashō was
so imbued with the spirit of Zen that it could not help
showing in everything he wrote. This is quite possibly
true, but as an explanation it suffers from the fact that
nobody has yet been able to define what the "spirit of
Zen" actually is. Zen "illumination" (*satori*) is apparently a strong emotional experience for which
there are no words. It has been called a "realizing of
reality," and some Christian theologians have praised
it as being "the highest form of natural mysticism."
About all that non-Zen people can do is to observe its
effects on Bashō and on his poems. Among the qualities which are often considered as indicative of his
Zen are a great zest for life; a desire to use every
instant to the uttermost; an appreciation of this even
in natural objects; a feeling that nothing is alone,
nothing unimportant; a wide sympathy; and an acute
awareness of relationships of all kinds, including that
of one sense to another. Whether or not these qualities
are due to Zen, they do exist in Bashō's haiku, at
least in the originals.

Only comparatively few of Bashō's poems are obviously religious, though several seem to be records of
semi-mystic experiences. For example, in his *Sarashina
Journey* Bashō records that while he and his pupil
Etsujin were journeying through the mountains of
Kiso, they found themselves climbing a steep and
dangerous path. On their left was a deep gorge, and
at its bottom, thousands of feet below, a rushing river.
They took each step in terror, until they came to the
fragile ivy-covered rope bridge which spanned the
gorge and which they had to cross. Bashō gives no details of his feelings, but appends the haiku:

Around existence twine
(Oh, bridge that hangs across the gorge!)
ropes of twisted vine.

There are also other poems, which would be obviously religious to a Japanese Buddhist of any sect:

Octopus traps: how soon
they are to have an end—these dreams
beneath the summer moon.

Octopus traps are earthenware pots, set horizontally in shallow water, into which during the nighttime the animal backs as if it were a crevice in the rocks. In the morning it is unable to get out. In the original, which is prefaced with the words: "On board a boat," the effect of *wo* is to make the moon the subject, and suggest that it looks down on the whole sea- and landscape, and all its "ephemeral dreams." Here the religious implications are obvious, even if we do not go into the Buddhist symbolism of the boat and the moon. It is, however, worthy of note that whenever Bashō uses the word "dream" he seems also to be thinking of human life; and perhaps it is even more noteworthy that to him the "illusion" of the world does not seem to mean that it is in any sense unreal, but rather, as with St. Thomas Aquinas, that it is far more real than it seems.

Kakehashi | *ya* | *inochi* | *wo* | *karamu* | *tsuta-katsura*
Hanging-bridge | : | life | [acc.] | entwine | ivy-vines

One interpretation of the rather cryptic phrase "*inochi wo karamu*" is that the very vines are hanging on for dear life.

Taka-tsubo | *ya* | *hakanaki* | *yume* | *wo* | *natsu-no-tsuki*
Octopus-pots | : | ephemeral | dreams | [onto] | summer-moon

The vast majority of Bashō's haiku are not obviously religious, whatever the Zen content may be. They are for the most part simple descriptions of actual scenes and events, with just enough detail given to allow the reader to put himself in Bashō's place and so share his emotions. Unfortunately many of the poems contain references which, although perfectly clear to those he was writing for, are meaningless to most foreigners, and so have to be omitted here. I cannot, however, resist giving one which is my own special favorite:

> In all the rains of May
> there is one thing not hidden—
> the bridge at Seta Bay.

The "Long Bridge" at Seta is one of the famous "Eight Views of Lake Ōmi," and would be known to almost every Japanese; at least some foreigners know it through Hiroshige's prints. It is built on piles, and crosses the southern end of Lake Ōmi where it narrows and forms a shallow bay, which overflows into a little river. When Bashō wrote this poem he probably saw the bridge from much the same point of view as Hiroshige did—and as I have been lucky enough to see it—across the water from the river edge. The bridge, however, is so long that in heavy rain, from whatever point of view it is seen, not more than one end could be visible; and, of course, behind it, unseen, are the other seven views.

This haiku may have inspired a quite possibly apocryphal story that Bashō was once asked, jokingly, to compose a haiku on all eight views. The point of the joke was that there did exist a well-known *tanka* (of thirty-one syllables) in which, by a series of word

Samidare-ni | *kakurenu* | *mono* | *ari* | *Seta-no-hashi*
May-rains-in | not-hidden | thing | there-is | Seta-bridge

plays, all eight views actually are mentioned by name. This was manifestly impossible to do in seventeen syllables, but the story goes that Bashō got out of the trap by answering:

> Eight Views?—Ah, well;
>   mist hid seven when I heard
>   Mii-dera's bell.

The "Bell of Mii Temple," considered to have a surpassingly lovely sound, is of course one of the so-called "Views."

In addition to the *Sarashina Kikō*, Bashō wrote several other prose works. The most famous of these is *Oku-no-Hosomichi, Narrow Roads in Oku*, a collection of notes of a six months' journey which started from Edo in the spring of 1689, went through parts of northern Japan, and ended at the sacred shrine of the Sun Goddess at Ise. It is quite short and contains only about fifty of his haiku. Yet it is undoubtedly one of the great works of Japanese literature, and it has probably been annotated and commented on more than any other work of its size in the world. Comment is unfortunately often necessary as Bashō's prose is, like his poetry, extremely condensed, and he is constantly making allusions that were clear in his own day, but which are not clear now.*

Even the title has been the subject of controversy, partly because *michi* (road) may be either singular or plural, and partly because the word *oku*, which is

* An excellent English translation has been made by Dr. Donald Keene, part of which is given in his *Anthology of Japanese Literature*, Vol. I.

Shichi | kei | wa | kiri-ni | kakurete | Mii-no-kane
Seven | views | as-for | mist-in | being-hidden | Mii's bell

an epithet applied to the northern provinces, has a
basic meaning something like that of "the interior."
The same point comes up in one of the poems, where
a song of "*oku*" is contrasted to the sophisticated art of
the cities (*fūryū*). Bashō is reporting a conversation
held shortly after his entering the "*oku*" country:

"My host asked first: 'At the crossing of the Shira-
kawa Barrier, what poem did you compose?'

"The troubles of the long journey had tired me in
body and mind, and moreover, I was carried away by
the scenery and the old-time feeling that it evoked, so
that I was not in any condition to compose a poem at
the moment. But thinking it a pity to pass in silence,
I made this one:

> The beginning of all art:
>   a song when planting a rice field
>   in the country's inmost part.

"I gave him this for an answer, and we added a second
and a third verse to it, and so made it into a *renga*
[a linked verse]."

Many pages of comment have been written about
this poem, and many explanations of it have been
given. One is that Bashō, coming as he did straight
from the ultra-refinement of Edo, was struck with the
fact that only rice culture made its luxury financially
possible. Another, that he was pointing out the
necessary connection between true refinement and
natural simplicity. A third is that Bashō was simply
paying a compliment to his host. The poem means different things to different people, and the reader may
take his choice.

Fūryū-no | *hajime* | *ya* | *oku-no* | *ta-ue-uta*
Refinement's | beginning | : | "interior's" |
rice-planting-song

Oku-no-Hosomichi contains several of Bashō's most famous poems, and also one can learn from it much about his character and what impelled him to compose. He tells us, for instance, how one day at the beginning of May he came to a certain village. At that time, in preparation for the Boys' Festival of the fifth day of the fifth month, every household with a boy in it would be flying, from the tops of tall flagpoles, great streamers of cloth or paper made to look like carp. Bashō does not say anything about this, as all Japanese would know it naturally, but among other things he tells how he went to the local temple and had tea there. He found that this temple preserved as its greatest treasures the sword of Yoshitsune, Japan's favorite hero, and the portable altar that used to be carried by the monk Benkei, the strong man who became Yoshitsune's most noted retainer. Bashō then inserts the haiku:

> Altar of Benkei,
>> Yoshitsune's sword! . . . Oh, fly
>> the carp in May!

a poem whose meaning may seem a little obscure at first, but which, though not deep, is charming after a little reflection.

And, then, a little later he comes to Takadate, the "Castle-on-the-Heights," where Yoshitsune and his last faithful followers were killed. From this spot he could see the plain of Hiraizumi, all green fields and wasteland, where in former ages the Fujiwara clans had lived in splendor. Bashō tells how he climbed up to the site of the castle, thinking of bygone glories, and,

Oi | *mo* | *tachi* | *mo* | *satsuki* | *ni* | *kazare* | *kami-nobori*
Altar | [too] | sword | [too] | May | in | decorate-[with] | paper-streamers

finding it only a wilderness of grass, sat down and wept. He then inserts the haiku:

> *Natsu-gusa ya*
> *tsuwamono-domo ga*
> *yume no ato.*

It is almost impossible to reproduce this in English, because we have no proper words. *Natsu-gusa* stands for all the quick-growing plants of summer; *tsu-wamono,* literally "the strong ones," was a name for medieval warriors, somewhat archaic even in Bashō's time; *-domo* is a plural suffix; *yume,* "dream," has overtones of "splendor" and of "lives like dreams"; and *ato,* a noun which basically means "after," includes the ideas of relic, trace, aftermath, what is left behind, etc. The most nearly literal English I can find is:

> Summer grasses:
> the afterward of strong men's dreams.

The original, however, conveys a strong sense of grief, due at least in part to the martial roll of *tsu-wamono-domo* and the crack of the following *ato.* Bashō, for all his gentleness and his Zen, was a samurai by birth, and was living in an age when samurai were no longer doing deeds of glory. I wish that some genius could find the proper English for this haiku. I myself have not been able to do so. After twenty-five years of trying, the best that I can do is:

> Summer grass:
> of stalwart warriors splendid dreams
> the aftermath.

Natsu-gusa | ya | tsuwamono-domo-ga | yume-no | ato
Summer-grasses | : | strong-ones' [plural] | dreams' | afterward

Immediately after this poem comes one by Sora,
Bashō's pupil and fellow traveler:

> In deutzia flowers there
>   one can see old Kanefusa—
>   snow-white hair!

The point of this is that the flowers of the *u* (the
Deutzia scabra, sometimes called the Japanese sun-
flower) are white, and Kanefusa, one of Yoshitsune's
retainers, was an old man with white hair. It is not a
very good poem, but it does illustrate one of the trains
of thought suggested by Bashō's haiku—a direct comparison between the grasses and the "dreams," both
of which grow and flower and die—and it is probable
that this is why Bashō included it.

Bashō's next haiku after the "summer grasses" is in
some ways its opposite and complement: it looks hope-
fully into the future instead of sadly into the past:

> Through all the fall
>   of June rains it still stands?
>   Oh, Shining Hall!

The "Shining Hall" was one of the "Golden Temples"
of Chūsonji, and one of the last remaining examples of
the splendors of the northern Fujiwara barons, who in
the twelfth century were almost independent princes.
It is small, but most gorgeously decorated. In the text
of *Oku-no-Hosomichi*, after describing the ravages of
wind and weather, Bashō reports that shortly before
his arrival this temple had been entirely enclosed in a

U-no-hana | *ni* | *Kanefusa* | *miyuru* | *shiraga* | *kana*
Deutzia-flowers | in | Kanefusa | gets-seen | white-hair |
kana

Samidare | *no* | *furi-nokoshite* | *ya* | *hikari-dō*
June-rain | 's | pouring-has-let-it-remain | ? | Shining-Hall

new outer construction so as to make it a memorial "for a thousand years." The wish has been nearly fulfilled, as the building, now well into its ninth century, is still standing.

Other haiku from *Oku-no-Hosomichi* are given in the poems that follow the text, but one more needs discussion here, because it requires a type of reader co-operation to which most foreigners are unaccustomed:

> Into the sea
>   it drives the red-hot sun—
>   the river Mogami.

In the prose text Bashō has previously told us that the time is summer, and that he has boarded a boat to go down the river, which is large and swift. But this information is not really needed to give a feeling of the welcome coolness after a hot day, and the rush of waters. And even a slight attempt to put ourselves into Bashō's position is enough to make us realize that he must be looking down the river, and westward across its mouth, to where the red ball of the sun is sinking into the waters. It is only after we have done this that we can begin to share in the emotions that prompted him to make the poem.

In 1694 Bashō died, and died as he would have wished, on one of his beloved wanderings, and surrounded by many of his friends and pupils. During his last illness he was constantly discussing religion and philosophy and poetry (three things that were almost one to Bashō), and when it became evident that he was dying his friends asked him to give them a "death poem"—the sum of his philosophy. Bashō refused, on the ground that every poem in his last ten years, start-

Atsuki | hi-wo | umi | ni | iretari | Mogami-gawa
Hot | sun [acc.] | sea | to | has-put-in | Mogami-river

ing with the "old pond" haiku, had been composed as
if it were a death poem. But on the next morning he
called them to his bedside, saying that during the
night he had dreamed, and that on waking a poem
had come to him. And he gave them:

> On a journey, ill,
>   and over fields all withered, dreams
>   go wandering still.

Surely as lovely a farewell as any poet ever gave to
the world.

The translations that follow are given with little or
no comment. But it might be well to remind the
beginner in haiku that though all these poems have
more to them than is on the surface, none of them are
allegories in the ordinary sense, and most of them are
primarily pictures. Abbé Dimnet * suggests that we
should all make notes of those experiences which we
should like to remember. These notes, he says, should
be "brief enough to preclude the danger of what the
Veda calls 'putting words between the truth and our-

---

* In *The Art of Thinking*, by Ernest Dimnet, Simon &
Schuster, N. Y., 1929.

*Tabi | ni | yamite | yume | wa | kare-no | wo |
kake-meguru*

Journey | on | taken-ill | dreams | as-for | dried-up-fields |
on | run-about

To get the force of *kakemeguru*, "go wandering" should
be given its most active sense. For those who wish to go
back to the original I must add that the word "still" is
used, not only because it seems definitely implied, but also
because of Bashō's subsequent reference, as reported in the
"Oi Nikki," to *nao kakameguru yume*, dreams which run
about "still" or "still more."

selves,' " and at the same time "full enough to be clear to future, i.e. almost alien, re-reading." If we consider Bashō's later haiku as notes of this kind in poetic form, we shall not go far wrong in our appreciation of them.

The Rice-Gourd

No rice?—in that hour,
   into the gourd we put
     a maiden-flower.

The Camellia

As it fell,
   water poured out—
     the camellia-bell.

Thin Shanks

Thin shanks! Even so,
   while I have them—blossom-covered
     hills of Yoshino!

Date not known	*Kome | no naki | toki | wa | hisago | ni | musume-hana*
	Rice | not-be | time | as-for | gourd | in | maiden-flower
Date not known	*Ochizama | ni | mizu | koboshi-keri | hana-tsubaki*
	Fall-way | in | water | spill-out-*keri* | flower-camellia
	This is the Japanese single camellia.
Date not known	*Yase-sune | mo | areba | zo | hana-no | Yoshino-yama*
	Thin-shanks | even | since-there-are | zo | flowery | Yoshino-mountain

The Unknown Flower

To bird and butterfly
  unknown, a flower blooms:
    the autumn sky.

Persistence

Did it yell
  till it became *all* voice?
    Cicada—shell!

Sudden Shower

Not even a hat—
  and cold rain falling on me?
    Tut-tut! think of that!

Date not known	*Chô* | *tori-no* | *shiranu* | *hana* | *ari* | *aki-no-sora*
	Butterfly | bird's | not-known | flower | there-is | autumn-sky

Date not known	*Koe* | *ni* | *mina* | *naki-shimaute* | *ya* | *semi-no-kara*
	Voice | to | all | crying-out | ? | cicada-shell

Date not known	*Kasa* | *mo* | *naki* | *ware* | *wo* | *shigururu ka* | *nanto-nanto*
	Hat | even | not | me | [on] | get-cold-rain? | what-not

New Year's Day

The first day of the year:
    thoughts come—and there is loneliness;
        the autumn dusk is here.

The Beginning

Spring starts:
    new year; old rice,
        five quarts.

Seen from Horseback

Near the road it flowered,
    the mallow—and by my horse
        has been devoured!

1684 *Ganjitsu* | *ya* | *omoeba* | *sabishi* | *aki-no-kure*
      Starting-day | : | when-think | be-lonely |
      autumn-nightfall
   New Year's Day is the beginning of spring, and normally
a time for happy thoughts.

1684 *Haru* | *tatsu* | *ya* | *shin-nen* | *furuki* | *kome* | *go* | *shō*
      Spring | starts | : | new-year | old | rice | five | shō

   A quart is somewhat smaller than a *shō*, so Bashō actually had over seven to start the new year. Bashō had
near the entrance of his house a gourd container into
which his pupils used to put presents of rice.

1684 *Michinobe-no* | *mukuge* | *wa* | *uma* | *ni* |
      kuware-keri
      Roadside | mallow | as-for | horse | by |
      was-eaten-*keri*

   In collections of Bashō's poems this usually has a foreword either *"Bajō no uta"* (Horseback poem), or *"Me no*

On the Road to Nara

Oh, these spring days!
A nameless little mountain,
    wrapped in morning haze!

On the Mountain Pass

Here on the mountain pass,
    somehow they draw one's heart so—
        violets in the grass.

---

mae" (Before my eyes). According to one report, it was this haiku that persuaded Bashō's final Zen teacher to accept him as a pupil. It is a strictly factual statement, not a moral fable. The particular mallow referred to is a rose of Sharon.

1685 *Haru | nare | ya | na-mo-naki | yama-no | asa-gasumi*

Spring | is-it | ? | name-even-not | mountain's | morning-mist

Nara is surrounded by famous mountains whose names are known to every educated Japanese. *Haru nare ya* is almost "Is it because of spring?"

1685 *Yama-ji | kite | naniyara | yukashi | sumire-gusa*

Mountain-path | coming | in-some-special-way | be-attractive | violet-plant

Naniyara conveys a feeling of wonder: "what can it be?" *Yukashi* suggests attractiveness based on simple fineness.

Leaving the House of a Friend

Out comes the bee
    from deep among peony pistils—
      oh, so reluctantly!

Clouds

Clouds come from time to time—
    and bring to men a chance to rest
      from looking at the moon.

The Autumn Storm

Wild boars and all
    are blown along with it—
      storm-wind of fall!

1685 *Bōtan-shibe | fukaku | wake-izuru | hachi-no | nagori | kana*
      Peony-pistil | deeply | part-and-go-out | bee's | reluctance | *kana*

1685 *Kumo | ori-ori | hito-ni | yasumuru | tsuki-mi | kana*
      Clouds | time-to-time | people-to | give-rest | moon-viewing | *kana*

1686 *Inoshishi | mo | tomo-ni | fukaruru | nowake | kana*
      Wild-boars | even | together-with | get-blown | autumn-storm | *kana*

Song from the Sky

The whole long day
  he sang, and is unsated still—
    the skylark.

In a Wide Wasteland

On the moor: from things
  detached completely—
    how the skylark sings!

On a Journey

Wake up! Wake up! It's I,
  who want you for companion,
    sleeping butterfly!

1687 *Nagaki | hi | wo | saezuri | taranu | hibari | kana*
      Long | day | *wo* | singing | not-be-enough |
      skylark | *kana*

The picture is of the lark, high up in the last rays of the
setting sun.

1687 *Hara-naka | ya | mono-ni-mo | tsuka-zu |
      naku-hibari*
      Moor-midst | : | thing-to-even | be-attached-not |
      singing-skylark

1687 *Oki-yo | oki-yo | waga | tomo | ni | semu | neru |
      kochō*
      Get-up! | Get-up! | my | companion | into |
      will-make | sleeping | butterfly

The Cuckoo

Little gray cuckoo:
  sing and sing; and fly and fly—
    Oh, so much to do!

The Harvest Moon

Harvest moon:
  around the pond I wander
    and the night is gone.

The Poor Man's Son

Poverty's child—
  he starts to grind the rice,
    and gazes at the moon.

1687 *Hototogisu* | *naki* | *naki* | *tobu* | *zo* | *isogawashi*
      Cuckoo | sing | sing | fly | !! | very-busy

1687 *Meigetsu* | *ya* | *ike* | *wo* | *megurite* | *yo-mo-sugara*
      Bright-moon | ! | pond | *wo* | go-around |
      night-already-over

1687 *Shizu-no* | *ko* | *ine-suri-kakete* | *tsuki* | *wo* | *miru*
      Poverty's child | rice-grind-starting | moon | at |
      looks

The Way of Zen

Well then, let's go—
    to the place where we tumble down
        looking at snow!

Near the Great Shrine, Ise

From what tree's bloom
    it comes, I do not know,
        but—this perfume!

Where the Cuckoo Flies

Where the cuckoo flies
    till it is lost to sight—out there
        a lone island lies.

1687 *Iza | yukamu | yuki-mi | ni | korobu | tokoro | made*
    Well | let's-go | snow-viewing | [in] | fall-down |
    place | up-to

Another version replaces *yukamu* with *saraba* (if it be
that way), indicating that the first suggestion to go snow-
viewing came from Bashō's friends.

1688 *Nan-no-ki-no | hana | to-wa | shirazu | nioi | kana*
    What-tree's | blossom | as-for-that | know-not |
    scent | *kana*

The Great Shrine is that of Amaterasu Ōmikami, the
Sun Goddess and Great Ancestor. The suggestion is that
the perfume may not be that of any actual tree.

1688 *Hototogisu | kie-yuku | kata | ya | shima | hitotsu*
    Cuckoo | vanish-go | direction | : | island | one

The End of Summer

The beginning of fall:
   the ocean, the rice fields—
      one green for all!

An Invitation to Etsujin

Snow that we two
   looked at together—this year
      has it fallen anew?

At the Grave of His Pupil Isshū

Grave mound, shake too!
   My wailing voice—
      the autumn wind.

1688   *Hatsu | aki | ya | umi | mo | aota-no | hito | midori*
       Starting | autumn | : | sea | also | rice-field's | one |
       green

1688   *Futari | mishi | yuki | wa | kotoshi | mo |
       furikeru ka*
       Two-people | looked-at | snow | [as-for] |
       this-year | also | has-fallen?

1688   *Tsuka | mo | ugoke | waga | naku | koe | wa |
       aki-no-kaze*
       Grave | too | shake [!] | my | crying | voice |
       as-for | autumn-wind

A *Painting of a Sake Drinker*

No blossoms and no moon,
  and he is drinking sake
    all alone!

The Stillness

So still:
  into rocks it pierces—
    the locust-shrill.

The Great River

All the rains of June
  it brings together, and is swift—
    the river Mogami.

1689   *Tsuki | hana | mo | nakute | sake | nomu | hitori | kana*

Moon | blossoms | also | not-being | sake | drink | alone | *kana*

1689   *Shizukasa | ya | iwa | ni | shimi-iru | semi-no-koe*

Stillness | : | rocks | to | pierce-in | locust-voices

From *Oku-no-Hosomichi*

1689   *Samidare | wo | atsumete | hayashi | Mogami-gawa*

Fifth-month-rain | [acc.] | gathering | is-swift | Mogami-river

From *Oku-no-Hosomichi*

The River of Heaven

So wild a sea—
  and, stretching over Sado Isle,
    the Galaxy . . .

Suma Beach in Autumn

Between the waves:
  mixed in with little shells,
    shreds of bush-clover.

The "Inn of the World"

At this same inn
  slept pleasure women too.
    Bush-clover and the moon!

1689 *Ara | umi | ya | Sado-ni | yokotau | Ama-no | -gawa*
      Rough | sea | : | Sado [above] | stretch-across |
      Heaven's | -river

From *Oku-no-Hosomichi*. Sado lies about forty miles
westward of the main island. The Japanese name for the
Milky Way, "Heaven's River," enormously helps the effect
of the original.

1689 *Nami-no-ma | ya | kogai | ni | majiru | hagi-no |
      chiri*
      Wave-intervals | : | small-shells | with | mix-in |
      bush-clover | rubbish

From *Oku-no-Hosomichi*. It follows a reference to the
loneliness of Suma Beach in autumn.

1689 *Hito-ie | ni | yujō | mo | netari | tsuki | to | hagi*
      Same-house | in | courtesans | also | slept | moon |
      and | bush-clover

From *Oku-no-Hosomichi*. It was written when Bashō
discovered the fact, on setting out the next morning.

The Monkey's Raincoat

The first cold showers pour.
　　Even the monkey seems to want
　　　　a little coat of straw.

A Cove at the "Lake of the Views"

From all four quarters
　　cherry petals blowing in
　　　　to Biwa's waters!

The Sun Path

The sun's way:
　　hollyhocks turn toward it
　　　　through all the rain of May.

1689　*Hatsu-shigure | saru | mo | ko-mino wo | hoshige-nari*

　　First-cold-rain | monkey | even | small-straw-coat | seems-to-want

1690　*Shihō | yori | hana | fuki-irete | Niō-no-umi*

　　"Four-directions" | from | blossoms | blowing-entering | Niō-Lake

Niō is a name given to Biwa or Ōmi, the lake of the "Eight Views."

Another version ends with "waves" instead of "lake."

1690　*Hi-no | michi | ya | aoi | katabuku | satsuki-ame*

　　Sun's | road | : | hollyhocks | lean-toward | fifth-month-rain

Summer Voices

So soon to die,
    and no sign of it is showing—
        locust cry.

A Cuckoo in the Old Capital

In Kyō I am,
    and still I long for Kyō—
        oh, bird of time!

1690 *Yagate* | *shinu* | *keshiki* | *wa* | *mie-zu* | *semi-no* |
      koe

      Soon | die | indication | as-for | appear-not |
      locust's | voices

The name of Bashō's young master Sengin means
"locust song."

1690 *Kyō* | *nite-mo* | *Kyō* | *natsukashi* | *ya* | *hototogisu*
      Kyō | though-being-in | Kyō | long-for | : | cuckoo

Kyō (Kyoto, founded A.D. 795), where the Emperor
lived, was the old capital. Wonderful as it was, and is, its
heyday was long past, and its glories were overshadowed
by Edo (now Tokyo), the seat of the Shoguns. In this
poem *hototogisu* is written with characters meaning "bird
of time."

Bamboo Grove

Song of the cuckoo:
  in the grove of great bamboos,
    moonlight seeping through.

A Wish

I'd like enough drinks
  to put me to sleep—on stones
    covered with pinks.

The Chestnut Burr

The winds of fall
  are blowing, yet how green
    the chestnut burr.

1691 *Hototogisu | ō-take | yabu-no | moru | tsuki-yo*
  Cuckoo | large-bamboo | thicket's | seep-in |
  moon-evening

Another version ends with *tsuki-zo,* which tends to over-emphasize the seeping of the moonlight rather than that of the cuckoo's song.

1691 *Youte | nemu | nadeshiko | sakeru | ishi-no | ue*
  Being-drunk | would-lie-down | pinks |
  bloomed-on | stone's | top

1691 *Aki-kaze-no | fuke-domo | aoshi | kuri-no-iga*
  Autumn-wind's | blowing-although | are-green |
  chestnut-burrs

Bush-Clover

Bush-clover does not spill
one small white dewdrop—though its waves
are never still.

Twilight

"Hawk-eyes too will fail,
now that the darkness comes"—
so chirp the quail.

1691   *Shira-tsuyu | mo | kobosanu | hagi-no | uneri | kana*
White-dew | even | not-let-fall | bush-clover's |
undulation | *kana*

Other versions have *wo* for *mo*, and *hito-tsuyu* (one
dewdrop) for *shira-tsuyu*. This translation is rather free, in
the belief that *uneri* refers more to waves like the waves of
a wheat field than to the actual curve of the branches
(cf. Issa's poem on p. 134), and that "dewdrop" has its
usual suggestion of short human life. There are many explanations of this poem, ranging from the highly religious
to the erotic.

1691   *Take-no | me | mo | ima | ya | kurenu | to |
naku-uzura*
Hawk's | eyes | too | now | [?] | darkened | thus |
chirping-quail

Beauty

The usually hateful crow:
  he, too—this morning,
    on the snow!

Harbingers

Spring too, very soon!
  They are setting the scene for it—
    plum tree and moon.

The Mushroom

The mushroom:
  from an unknown tree, a leaf
    sticks to it.

1691   *Higoro | nikumu | karasu | mo | yuki-no-ashita | kana*
       Usually | hateful | crow | even | snow-y-morning | kana

1692   *Haru | mo | yaya | keshiki | totonou | tsuki | to | ume*
       Spring | also | soon | scene | prepare | moon | and | plum

1692   *Matsutake | ya | shiranu | ko-no-ha-no | hebarizuki*
       Mushroom | : | unknown | tree's-leaf's | sticking-on

Sent to His Pupil Ransetsu

Won't you come and see
loneliness? Just one leaf
from the *kiri* tree.

On New Year's Day

Spring that no man
has seen: plum bloom on the back
of the mirror.

1692 *Sahishisa* | *wo* | *toute* | *kurenu* | *ka* | *kiri* | *hito* | *ha*
Loneliness | [acc.] | visiting | will you not do | ? |
paulownia | one | leaf

The *kiri* (paulownia) is noted for dropping its leaves
even when no breath of wind is stirring.

1693 *Hito* | *mo* | *minu* | *haru* | *ya* | *kagami-no* | *ura-no* |
ume
Person | even | not-see | spring | : | mirror's |
back's | plum tree

Japanese bronze hand mirrors were usually decorated
with a raised design on the back, one favorite motif being
quite beautiful but highly stylized plum branches. It seems
unnecessary to drag in Shinto in order to explain the
almost world-wide feeling that there is something occult
about a mirror and what is behind it.

The Village Without Bells

A village where they ring
no bells!—Oh, what do they do
at dusk in spring?

Bell Tones

As bell tones fade,
blossom scents take up the ringing—
evening shade!

The Cuckoo's Song

As the cuckoo flies,
its singing stretches out:
upon the water lies.

1693   *Kane | tsukanu | mura | wa | nani | wo | ka |
haru-no-kure*

Bell | ring-not | village | as-for | what | [acc.] | ? |
spring-evening

1693   *Kane | kiete | hana-no | ka | wa | tsuku | yube |
kana*

Bell | fading-out | blossom's | scent | as-for | strike |
evening | *kana*

1693   *Hototogisu | koe | yokotau | ya | mizu-no | ue*

Cuckoo | voice | stretch-across | : | water's | top

The cuckoo flies horizontally, singing as it goes.

Mountain Plum Blossoms

With the scent of plums
  on the mountain road—suddenly,
    sunrise comes!

Coolness

How very cool it feels
  taking a noonday nap, to have
    a wall against my heels!

The Family

Leaning upon staves
  and white-haired—a whole family
    visiting the graves.

1694   *Ume-ga-ka | ni | notto | hi-no | deru | yama-ji |*
       kana

       Plums'-scent | in | suddenly | sun's | coming-out |
       mountain-road | *kana*

1694   *Hiya-hiya | to | kabe | wo | fumaete | hiru-ne | kana*

       Cool-cool | thus | wall | [acc.] | putting-foot-on |
       noon-sleep | *kana*

1694   *Ie | wa | mina | tsue-ni | shirage-no | haka-mairi*

       Family | as-for | all | staff-with | white-hair's |
       grave-visiting

There is another (earlier) version *"ikka mina shirage ni
tsue ya hakamairi."* Both versions are somewhat ambigu-
ous. The generally accepted picture seems to have been
that of a fairly large family, some of whom are very old.
Recent researches by Kikuyama Tane have, however,
thrown a new light on the poem. It refers to a visit to the

Lightning at Night

A lightning gleam:
    into darkness travels
        a night heron's scream.

The Autumn of Life

Nearing autumn's close,
    my neighbor, now—what is it
        that he does?

---

family graves made in Bashō's native village in remem-
brance of the recent death of Bashō's common-law wife.
There were present, in addition to Bashō himself, his wife's
mother (a very old lady), his two older brothers, and apparently their wives, and also his wife's brother. (Bashō's
two daughters were apparently still in Edo.) Who else
was there, we do not know, but the "whole household"
was quite small, and certainly for the most part made up of
elderly people. Bashō's oldest brother had no children, and
the second brother's oldest son, whom Bashō had adopted,
had died within the year. Bashō, as other poems of the
period indicate, was already looking forward to his own
death, and on this occasion was, it seems to me, looking
forward to the probable extinction of his whole family as
well.

1694   *Inazuma | ya | yami-no-kata-yuku | goi-no | koe*
        Lightning | : | darkness-direction-go |
        night-heron's | voice

1694   *Aki | fukaki | tonari | wa | nani | wo | suru | hito |
        zo*
        Autumn | deep | neighbor | as-for | what | [acc.] |
        do | person | *zo*

Bashō's Road

This road:
  with no man traveling on it,
    autumn darkness falls.

1694 *Kono | michi | ya | yuku-hito | nashi | ni |
      aki-no-kure*

      This | road | : | going-person | be-none | [with] |
      autumn-nightfall

Chapter IV

BASHŌ'S PUPILS

BASHŌ was so fond of people that naturally they, too, were fond of him. He had an uncounted number of friends and followers, and it is said that three hundred of his special pupils followed his body to the little country temple where he is buried near Lake Biwa. Of these special pupils there are ten in particular who carried on his methods during the early part of the eighteenth century. These men were known as the "Ten Philosophers," a name that was derived from that of the ten pupils of Confucius, but which does not necessarily indicate that they are really to be regarded as philosophers rather than as poets.

The list of their names is as follows: Etsujin, Hokushi, Jōsō, Kikaku, Kyorai, Kyoroku, Ransetsu, Shikō, Sanpū, Yaha. Etsujin survived his teacher for only eight years, dying in 1702, while the last of them, Yaha, lived until 1740. In general they were all competent poets and fair philosophers, and most of them founded schools of their own, but their work seldom reached the standard set by the genius of Bashō.

The two most famous of the Ten Philosophers are Ransetsu (1653–1708) and Kikaku (1661–1707). From the Japanese point of view Ransetsu was probably the finest of them all. As an example of what Bashō's teaching had accomplished, it is interesting to compare the feeling and the philosophy of his poem on dewdrops:

> Play about, do,
> from grass-leaf to grass-leaf!
> Jewels of dew!

with that of Sōin (page 13). The comparison of dew to our short human lives is suggested in both of them, but from very different points of view.

Another poem, in which internal emotions are well expressed by a simple description of an external scene is:

> New Year's Day:
> clouds dispersed, and sparrows
> chattering away.

In Japan, it should be noted, New Year's Day is a very happy season, and has attached to it some of the feeling that we associate with Christmas.

Ransetsu's most famous haiku, however, is the following almost untranslatable poem on early spring:

Kusa-no-ha | wo | asobiarike | yo | tsuyu-no-tama
Grass-leaves | [acc.] | play-among | ! | dew-jewels

Ganjitsu | ya | harete | suzume-no | monogatari
New Year's Day | : | being-clear | sparrows' | talking-about-things

On the plum tree
one blossom, one blossomworth
of warmth.

On the surface this is simply a picture of the first
signs of the breakup of winter. But it is also a balance
of ideas, and hence a starting point for trains of
thought. To anyone who has lived through the nastily
cold winters of Japan and seen the warm pink of the
early plum blossoms, appropriate ideas come naturally
enough. There is the suggestion that with the second
blossom there will come another blossom-equivalent
of warmth, with the third a third, etc., and vice-versa,
so that one could translate it:

As on the plums
blossom by blossom, so too
spring warmness comes.

But one could make a thousand other versions also:

On the plum is glowing
one blossom; now one blossom strong,
warmth too is growing.

or:

On the plum, forlorn,
one blossom; one frail blossomworth
of warmth has just been born.

etc., etc., etc.

All of these versions would probably be right, each
from its own point of view, and all of them would
certainly be wrong, as each would give one point of
view only. It is not to be supposed that Ransetsu con-

Ume | *ichi* | *rin* | *ichi* | *rin* | *hodo-no* | *atatakasa*
Plums | one | bloom | one | bloom | extent's | warmth

sciously thought out all the versions possible. Of
course he did not, and probably no two people will
get quite the same meaning out of his poem. Nevertheless—indeed partly because of this fact—this is
haiku of the very first grade. How popular it is may
be judged from the fact that some years ago an
hour's talk on the exact meaning of this poem was
given over the radio.

Among the "Ten Philosophers" the one most consciously different from Bashō was Kikaku (1661–
1707). He was seventeen years younger than his
master, and in some ways never outgrew a childish
delight in playing the *enfant terrible*. He was nevertheless an acute observer, taking obvious delight in
seeing things that others had missed. Japanese critics
have contrasted his robust masculinity with the almost
feminine gentleness of Bashō. He was perhaps at his
best in such poems as the following description of a
naked beggar:

> There a beggar goes!
> Heaven and earth he's wearing
> for his summer clothes.

But in this, as in all his poems that I have read, he
seems to be looking at things from the outside, instead
of being in close sympathy with them, as Bashō is.
Where Bashō saw first of all the "Buddha-nature" of
things, Kikaku was interested in their own nature. He
was before everything else an observer, and in his
haiku otherworldliness usually comes in a bad second.
Take for example:

Kojiki | kana | tenchi | wo | kitaru | natsu-goromo
Beggar | *kana* | Heaven-and-Earth | [acc.] | is-wearing |
summer-clothes

> The cock again
>   is fighting like a lion:
>   see his mane!

Here there is little doubt that Kikaku is more interested in one particular cock than in cocks in general, and in this world more than in eternity.

Kyorai * reports that Bashō once said that Kikaku "could express inconsequential things beautifully"; but at other times the master praised him highly, and it should not be taken as necessarily implying that all of Kikaku's poems have only surface meaning. Such a haiku as:

> Dragonflies:
>   all their frenzies quiet down—
>   the young moon in the skies!

is obviously more than just a picture of dragonflies at dusk, and a poem like:

> The dawn is here:
>   and ho!—out of peach bloom the voice
>   of Chanticleer.

---

* In *Conversations with Kyorai*. An excellent though incomplete translation is given in Dr. Keene's *Anthology of Japanese Literature*.

Niwatori | *no* | *shishi-ni* | *hataraku* | *sakage* | *kana*
Cock | [subj.] | lion-as | strives | on-end-feathers | *kana*

Seirei | *ya* | *kurui* | *shizumaru* | *mika-no* | *tsuki*
Dragonflies | : | wild-behavior | become-quiet |
three-day's | moon

Akebono | *ya* | *koto-ni* | *tōka-no* | *tori-no* | *koe*
Daybreak | : | especially | peach-bloom's | cock's | voice

is more than simply a description of daybreak; though here indeed Kikaku's chief interest seems to have been to paint a "Symphony in Reds." *

On the other hand Kikaku did sometimes act like a spoiled brat, and liked to show off his cleverness by being deliberately different from his elders—sometimes to such an extent as to draw gentle rebukes from Bashō. This propensity occasionally resulted in excellent poems, but also occasionally produced an air of insincerity. His well-known poem:

> In a dream she came,
>> my mother—and you send her back?
>> Cuckoo!

is clever in many ways, and not least in the suggestion of being waked by the "bird of the Other World." Yet one cannot help having the feeling that it was not written because of his love for his mother, but rather from a desire to be different from other poets, who were always praising the beauty of the cuckoo's song.

It seems to me that this desire to be different should be looked for in Kikaku's other haiku also. For instance, this one, on the harvest moon:

---

* Blyth (*Haiku*, Vol. II, page 195) has suggested that "*tōka-no tori*"—an unusual designation—may refer to a special "peach-blossom cock" obscurely mentioned in Chinese literature, who gave the signal to all other cocks. Certainly Kikaku, who enjoyed the unusual, might well have made such a reference. I feel sure that, if he did, he hoped that dull wights like me could see only the color.

Yume | *ni* | *kuru* | *haha* | *wo* | *kaesu* | *ka* | *hototogisu*
Dream | in | come | mother | [acc.] | send-back | ? | cuckoo

> Bright the full moon shines:
> on the matting of the floor,
> shadows of the pines.

Many consider this poem as primarily a picture of beauty, based on the contrast of the white moonlight and the black shadows that form a pattern with the black edging of the mats.* If anyone else had written it, one might accept it as simply giving a picture and the mood that goes with it. But here Kikaku certainly brings out the fact that he is enjoying the harvest moon indoors—while other people would normally be out "moon-viewing."

The poem that is often considered to be Kikaku's comment on human life is:

> { A tree frog, clinging
>   to a banana leaf—
>   and swinging, swinging. }

It might well be considered a comment on his own poetic life, especially when we remember that "banana leaf" (*bashō*) was the name of his master. Kikaku is more nearly on our own level than Bashō is, and so cannot lift us to such heights as he does, nor lead our thoughts so far. He seems more interested in accidental relationships than in basic ones. Nevertheless, he was always a poet, and the reader of his poems

---

* *Tatami* are thick straw mats, built on wooden frames, which form the flooring of most Japanese rooms. They are rectangles, about 6' x 3', with taped edges, usually black. The matting itself is a natural light straw color.

Meigetsu | ya | tatami-no | ue | ni | matsu-no-kage
Bright-moon | : | floor-mats' | top | on | pine-tree-shadows

Ama-gaeru | bashō | ni | norite | soyogi-keri
Rain-frog | banana-leaf | on | riding | swinging . . .

often feels, as Dr. Johnson phrases it, what he remembers to have felt before, but he feels it with a great increase of sensibility.

New Year's Greeting

The warbler, swinging
his body upside down,
 does his first singing.

At the Back of the Buddha (Kamakura)

The Great Buddha!—oh,
his lap must be all filled with it—
 cherry-blossom snow!

Outside the Sliding Door

The chirps of baby sparrows:
upon the paper of the door
 dwarf-bamboo shadows.

Uguisu-no | *saka-sama-ni* | *hatsune* | *kana*
Warbler's | upside-down-ly | first-singing | *kana*

Ō-botoke | *hiza* | *uzumuramu* | *hana-no-yuki*
Great-Buddha | lap | may-be-filled | blossom-snow

Suzume-go | *ya* | *akari-shōji-no* | *sasa-no* | *kage*
Baby-sparrows | : | translucent-sliding-door's |
dwarf-bamboos' | shadows

The Butterfly

A sleeping butterfly!
  During the nights,
    what can it be he does?

The Mournful Chirping

Eaten by the cat!
  Perhaps the cricket's widow
    may be bewailing that!

Summer Lightning

Lightning-play—
  that yesterday was in the east,
    is in the west today.

Neburu | *chō* | *yoru-yoru* | *nani* | *wo* | *suru* | *koto* | *zo*
Sleeping | butterfly | nights | what | [acc.] | do | things | ?!

Neko | *ni* | *kuwareshi* | *wo* | *kōrogi-no* | *tsuma* | *sudakuramu*
Cat | by | was-eaten | [acc.] | cricket's | wife | may-bewail

Inazuma | *ya* | *kinō* | *wa* | *higashi* | *kyō* | *wa* | *nishi*
Lightning | : | yesterday | as-for | east | today | as-for | west

Summer Evening

How cool things are:
  the coolest—on Musashi Plain
    a falling star.

Snow

"My snow!"—when I think that,
  it weighs almost nothing
    on my umbrella-hat!

More space is given here to Kikaku than to any of
the other pupils, not because of any considered judgment of his relative importance, but simply because I
like him. It is not possible to consider the rest of the
Ten Philosophers separately, but at least one poem
from each of them is given for comparison. None of
the poems seems to need much comment, except the
first one, by Etsujin, which is open to more than one
interpretation, as it is not stated who "comes to say."
The poem itself suggests that the one questioned is an
old man, musing on the melancholy thoughts that go
with autumn twilights. The feeling of many commentators that the one who comes must be the wife
who has grown old with him is strongly supported by
what is known about the poet.

Suzushisa | *ya* | *mazu* | *Musashi-no-no* | *nagare-boshi*
Coolness | : | in-first-place | Musashi-Plain's | shooting star

Musashi Plain is known for its great extent, unusual in
the mountainous country of Japan.

Waga | *yuki* | *to* | *omoeba* | *karushi* | *kasa-no* | *ue*
My | snow | thus | when-think | is-light | straw-hat's | top

Autumn Nightfall

Autumn, end of day;
   "Shall I light the lamp now?"
     someone comes to say.
   ETSUJIN (1656?–1739)

Nighttime

From the insects' tune
   surely it must be nighttime.
     Harvest moon!
   ETSUJIN

Year's End

Now this year goes away:
   I've kept it hidden from my parents
     that my hair is gray.

   ETSUJIN

Aki-no-kure | *hi* | *tomosan* | *to* | *toi-ni* | *kuru*
Autumn-nightfall | lamp | shall-I-light | thus | to-ask | comes

Mushi-no-oto | *de* | *satewa* | *yoru* | *nari* | *kyō-no* | *tsuki*
Insect-sounds | from | surely | night | it-is | today's | moon

Yukutoshi | *ya* | *oya-ni* | *shiraga* | *wo* | *kakushi-keri*
Departing-year | : | parents-from | white-hair | [acc.] |
have-kept-hidden

The Little Duck

"I've just come from a place
    at the lake bottom!"—*that* is the look
        on the little duck's face.

JŌSŌ (1661–1704)

The Barley Field

Bent down by the rain,
    the ripe barley makes this
        such a narrow lane!

JŌSŌ

Winter

Mountains and plains,
    all are captured by the snow—
        nothing remains.

JŌSŌ

Mina-soko | *wo* | *mite* | *kita* | *kao-no* | *kogamo* | *kana*
Water-bottom | [acc.] | seeing | have-come | face's |
little-duck | *kana*

Ame-ni | *orete* | *homugi-ni* | *semaki* | *komichi* | *kana*
Rain-by | bent-over | ripe-barley-by | narrow | path | *kana*

No-mo | *yama-mo* | *yuki ni* | *torareta* | *nanimo* | *nashi*
Plains-too | mountains-too | snow-by | have-been-taken |
everything | is-not

Cuckoo and Skylark

The cuckoo's cry,
  with the skylark's singing—
    a cross-mark on the sky.

KYORAI (1651–1704)

Enigma

Head or tail,
  which is which, one can't be sure—
    sea snail!

KYORAI

Melons

They rolled out too far
  from their leaf shelter, melons—
    and how hot they are!

KYORAI

Hototogisu | naku | ya | hibari | to | jūmonji
Cuckoo | singing | : | skylark | with | cross-mark

The cuckoo's flight is horizontal, that of the skylark straight up. (Ct. Bashō's poem, p. 48)

O-kashira-no | kokoromoto | naki | namako | kana
Head-and-tail's | sure-decision | is-not | sea snail | *kana*

Ha-gakure | wo | kokedete | uri-no | atsusa | kana
Leafy-hiding | [acc.] | rolling-out | melons' | heat | *kana*

Morning Prayers

Matin time—
    it's now that morning-glories
      reach their prime.

KYOROKU (1656–1715)

The Autumn Storm

First of all,
    it blows a scarecrow down—
      storm-wind of fall!

KYOROKU

Old Men's Tales

"Now many years ago . . ."
    tales of earthquakes being told
      round the brazier's glow.

KYOROKU

Kankin-no | *ma* | *wo* | *asagao-no* | *sakari* | *kana*
Morning-prayer's | interval | [acc.] | morning-glory's |
at-best | *kana*

Ichiban-ni | *kagashi* | *wo* | *taosu* | *nowaki* | *kana*
Number-one-at | scarecrow | [acc.] | make-fall |
autumn-storm | *kana*

Ima | *wa* | *mukashi* | *jishin* | *wo* | *kataru* | *hibachi* | *kana*
Now | as-for | long-ago | earthquakes | [acc.] | talk-of |
brazier | *kana*

The Summons

Banked fires; night grows late—
  then comes a sound of rapping
    at the gate.

KYOROKU

Moon-Viewing

The moon on the pine:
  I keep hanging it—taking it off—
    and gazing each time.

HOKUSHI (1665?–1718)

Maple Leaves

Envied by us all,
  turning to such loveliness—
    red leaves that fall.

SHIKŌ (1664–1731)

Umorebi | *ya* | *yo* | *fukete* | *mon* | *wo* | *tataku* | *oto*
Banked-fires | : | night | growing-late | gate | [acc.] |
knock-at | sound

Tsuki-wo | *matsu-ni* | *kakitari* | *hazushi* | *temo* | *mitari*
Moon [acc.] | pine-tree-on | hanging-on | taking-off |
and-still | looking-at

Urayamashi | *utsukushiu* | *natte* | *chiru* | *momiji*
Enviable | beautiful | becoming | falling | red-leaves

The Silver Lining

May rains pour:
  and now the frogs are swimming
    at my door!

SANPŪ (1647–1732)

Sparklings

Up they swing,
  and the mattocks glitter:
    fields in spring.

SANPŪ

The Seasons

Cherry-bloom, cuckoo,
  moon, snow—and already
    the year is through!

SANPŪ

Samidare-ni | kawazu-no | oyogu | toguchi | kana
May-rains-in | frogs' | swim | entrance-door | kana

Furiagaru | kuwa-no | hikari | ya | haru-no-nora
Swing-up | hoes' | glitter | : | spring-field

Hana | hototogisu | tsuki | yuki | mohaya | toshi-no | kure
Blossoms | cuckoo | moon | snow | already | year's | ending

The Umbrella

Come and pass and go—
one umbrella—only one—
evening, and the snow.

YAHA (1662–1740)

Bashō's other pupils beside the Ten Philosophers can here be given only passing mention. As a general statement it may be said that they were inferior to the Ten, and that too many of their poems seem to be made up of Bashō and water. The following are fair examples:

When no wind at all
disturbs the kiri tree—
the leaves that fall!

which is simply a weakening down of Bashō's message to Ransetsu (p. 47); and

To raging winds
companion:—in the sky
the single moon.

which seems obviously inspired by the "River of Heaven" haiku. It is rather interesting to compare the

Karakasa-no | *hitotsu* | *sugiyuku* | *yuki-no* | *kure*
Umbrella's | one | pass-by | snow-y | nightfall

Kiri-no-ki-no | *kaze-ni* | *kamawanu* | *ochiba* | *kana*
Paulownia-tree's | wind-by | not-disturbed | falling-leaves | *kana*

Fuku-kaze-no | *aite* | *ya* | *sora-no* | *tsuki* | *hitotsu*
Blowing-winds' | companion | : | sky's | moon | one

poems, and to observe the difficulty of consciously
trying to imitate Bashō.

Bonchō (d. 1714), who wrote these haiku, was one
of the better-known pupils, and by no means a bad
poet, though very irregular. He could write verses
like:

> See my razor, pray:
>> in one night it has rusted.
>> Oh, this rain of May.

which seem to me to be more like *senryū* than real
haiku. (*Senryū* are humorous poems in haiku form,
often more than slightly vulgar.) One the other hand,
his most famous poem has in the original a weirdly
haunting quality based on the almost universal feeling
that we are "homeless in our homes, and strangers
under the sun":

> Something makes a sound!
>> With no one near, a scarecrow
>> has fallen to the ground.

Whatever the shortcomings of the translation may be,
it can be said with truth that the original, with its suggestion of unseen powers about us, is capable of
making cold shivers run down one's spine.

Some of the other pupils also wrote very good
poems, but it is seldom that they strike any new note.
Izen's (1646–1711).

Kamisori | *ya* | *hito* | *yo* | *ni* | *sabite* | *go-gatsu-ame*
Razor | : | one | night | in | rusting | fifth-month-rain

Mono-no | *oto* | *hitori* | *taoruru* | *kagashi* | *kana*
Thing's | sound | alone | get-a-tumble | scare-crow | *kana*

Blooms on the plum,
  redder and redder and still
    redder they come!

is different from the usual style, but seems simply to
have been inspired by Onitsura rather than by Bashō.
I have not made any study of these minor poets, but
add a few examples of their work which I have happened to come across and to like.

The Barley Field

Up the barley rows,
  stitching, stitching them together,
    a butterfly goes.

SORA (1648–1710)

Dawn

Dawnlight, and from the well
up comes the bucket—in it
a camellia-bell.

KAKEI (1648–1716)

Ume-no-hana | *akai* | *wa* | *akai* | *wa* | *akai* | *kana*
Plum-blossoms | red | as-for | red | as-for | red | *kana*

Kurikaeshi | *mugi-no-une* | *nuu* | *kochō* | *kana*
Again-and-again | barley-rows | stitching | butterfly | *kana*

Akatsuki-no | *tsurube-ni* | *agaru* | *tsubaki* | *kana*
Dawnlight's | well-bucket-in | come-up | camellia | *kana*

Presumably, the camellia is a red one.

The Cuckoo

A cuckoo's cry:
  and today—just today—
    there is nobody by.

SHŌHAKU (1649–1722)

The "Rain-Frogs"

The tree frogs sing:
  and on the young leaves, suddenly
    a raindrop-pattering.

ROGETSU (1666–1751)

Hototogisu | *kyō-ni* | *kagirite* | *dare-mo* | *nashi*
Cuckoo | today-at | only | every-one | is-not

Amagaeru | *naku* | *ya* | *wakaba-no* | *tōri-ame*
Rain-frogs | singing | : | young-leaves' | passing shower

Chapter V

OTHER EARLY
EIGHTEENTH-CENTURY
POETS

Bashō and his school did not at once dominate the
field. Sōin's pupils and followers, known as the Danrin
School, were for some time a powerful body, and even
verses in Teitoku style were being manufactured in
large quantities. Then there were minor bodies, like
Onitsura's Itami School, and also a number of other
poets whose work did not wholly conform to that of
any recognized group.

One of the most interesting and individual of all the
haiku poets was Onitsura (1660–1738), whose light
was for a long time dimmed by the greater brightness
of Bashō. Like Bashō, he was of samurai birth and
started composing at an early age. Also like Bashō,
he resigned a lucrative post in order to devote himself to poetry—indeed he seems to have resigned two
or three such posts. He began his study of haiku under
Sōin when he was fifteen. While still a young man he
learned to have a high conception of a poet's duty,
and made the well-known statement: *"Makoto no
hoka ni haikai nashi,"* which means, approximately,

"Outside of truth there is no poetry." In typical Onitsura fashion, he reinforced this with an adage in haiku form:

> To get to know plum blossoms,
>   both one's own heart
>   and one's own nose.

Another of Onitsura's quotable remarks was made to the priest Kūdō. He was visiting the old gentleman, presumably having tea with him, when his host asked to be enlightened as to the nature of the poetic eye. Onitsura's answer, given on the spur of the moment, was:

> In the garden, see—
>   how whitely it is blooming,
>   the camellia tree.

all of which is in accordance with the best traditions. But after all, there were other poets who might have given a similar answer. On the other hand, no one but Onitsura would have been capable of such a shout of joy as:

> Cherry blossoms, more
>   and more now! Birds have two legs!
>   Oh, horses have four!

Ume | wo | shiru | kokoro | mo | onore | hana | mo | onore
Plums | [acc.] | get-to-know | heart | too | one's-own | nose | too | one's-own

Teizen | ni | shiroku | saitaru | tsubaki | kana
Garden | in | whitely | be-blooming | camellia | *kana*

Sakura | saku | koro | tori | ashi | ni | hon | uma | shi | hon
Cherries | bloom | time | birds | legs | two | piece | horses | four | piece

Such a clearing of the vision, so that we suddenly see and rejoice in ordinary things, is an experience probably common to all of us. But what other poet has ever expressed it so compactly and completely?

It is a pity that many of Onitsura's poems fail to give a clear picture and are rather too philosophical. In other words, they become more like epigrams than normal haiku should. The following example of the type was presented to the Abbot Daishin of Daitoku-ji on the occasion of his sixtieth birthday:

> Obedience is here:
>   even the silent flowers
>   speak to the inmost ear.

The point of it is that the sixtieth year was known as that of the "obedient ear," from a saying of Confucius that "at sixty the ear becomes obedient." It is included here chiefly because one of my most prized possessions is a Zen painting made by the abbot, who must have been a most delightful person.

Onitsura's best-known poem is:

> On top of skeletons
>   they put a gala dress, and then—
>   the flower-viewing!

On the face of it this is simply a cynical description of the revelers who put on their best clothes for the

Shitagau | *ya* | *oto-naki* | *hana* | *mo* | *mimi-no* | *oku*
Obeying | : | sound-less | flowers | even | ear's | inmost-part

Gaikotsu-no | *ue* | *ni* | *yosoute* | *hana-mi* | *kana*
Skeleton's | top | on | dress-up-and | flower-viewing | *kana*

cherry-viewing festival, and go out to see and be seen, with the implied suggestion that there is only a difference of degree between the shortness of human life and that of the cherry blossoms. Many critics have seen nothing else in the poem, and have dismissed it as not worthy of being called haiku. This reading, however, somehow seems out of keeping with what we know about Onitsura's character.

The poem has a rather cryptic foreword: *Bonnō areba shujō ari;* as far as I know, the point of it has never been made clear. The nearest English equivalent seems to be: "When there are worldly passions there are living beings." Leaving the foreword aside for the moment, and rereading the poem itself, one sees that Onitsura has left it to the reader to decide who does the dressing up, and that his description could apply to the cherry trees just as much as to the people—rather better, in fact, as the blossoms come out on practically leafless branches. A reading of his other poems shows that he, like many poets, quite often made a sort of equation between human beings and inanimate objects. If we make the equation here, and ascribe to the trees the same feelings that the people have—including that of taking pride in their fine appearance—we get a haiku, and a quite charming one. And furthermore, we can find a real point to the foreword.

Onitsura looked at life with a whimsical humor all his own, and his guiding principle seems to have been that what one gets one has to pay for—but it's worth it! The following haiku on the harvest moon is typical, and like several others, might well be entitled *Value Received:*

Mountains and plains,
look—as if it were noontime!
Of course one's neck pains.

Onitsura published his first book of poems when he
was nineteen, and wrote constantly from that time on,
though only about seven hundred of his verses have
been preserved. He was the recognized leader of
poetry in his home province and had considerable influence on other poets also, even on those who lived
in the capital. Needless to say, he was a great admirer
of his older contemporary, Bashō, though he wisely
refrained from copying Bashō's style, for which he
was temperamentally unfitted. The haiku:

Wandering dreams: alas,
over fields all burned, the wail
of winds that pass.

was composed for the great memorial gathering on
the thirteenth anniversary of Bashō's death, and of
course refers to Bashō's last poem (page 30).

At the age of seventy-three Onitsura retired from
the world, shaved his head, and entered the priest-
hood. From that time until his death five years later
he wrote no more poems, his last haiku being composed at the time he took the tonsure. It is an act of
renunciation:

No | mo | yama | mo | hiru | ka | to | zo | kubi-no | daruku | koso
Plains | too | mountains | too | noon | ? | thus | ! | neck's | aching | indeed

Kakemeguru | yume | ya | yake-no-no | kaze-no | oto
Wander-about | dreams | : | burned-fields' | winds' | sound

Chrysanthemums, all sere,
   that long ago were seventeen—
     my offering here!

Here "seventeen" refers not only to the number of
syllables in a haiku, but also has a conventional meaning of "young and lovely," like our "sweet sixteen";
flowers are used before most Buddhist altars.

Onitsura's First Poem (Age 8)

Although I say,
   "Come here! Come here!" the fireflies
     keep flying away!

Bush Warbler and Plum

The bush warbler—oh,
   his perchings on the plum tree
     started long ago!

Kare | *kiku* | *ya* | *mukashi* | *jūshichi* | *tamuke-gusa*
Dry | chrysanthemums | : | of-old | seventeen |
offering-flowers

Koi | *koi* | *to* | *iedo* | *hotaru* | *ga* | *tonde* | *yuku*
Come! | Come! | thus | say-although | fireflies | [subj.] |
flying | go

Uguisu | *ya* | *ume* | *ni* | *tomaru* | *wa* | *mukashi* | *kara*
Bush warbler | : | plum | in | perching | as-for | long-past |
from

There is in this a mildly "literary" reference, which takes
one's mind back to the ancient poets, who for more than
a thousand years had associated the two.

Cherry Blossoms

They blossom, and then
  we gaze, and then the blooms
    scatter, and then . . .

The Little Valley in Spring

A mountain stream:
  even the stones make songs—
    wild cherry trees.

Mii Temple

Blossoms go
  and again it's quiet
    at Onjō.

Saku | *kara-ni* | *miru* | *kara-ni* | *hana-no* | *chiru* | *kara-ni*
Blossom | after-at | look | after-at | blossom's | fall | after-at

Tani-mizu | *ya* | *ishi* | *mo* | *uta* | *yomu* | *yama-zakura*
Valley-water | : | stones | even | songs | compose | mountain-cherries

Hana | *chitte* | *mata* | *shizuka* | *nari* | *Onjō-ji*
Blossoms | falling | again | quiet | it-is | Onjō-Temple

Onjō is another name for Mii, the temple whose bell is one of the "Eight Views of Lake Ōmi."

Directions

Eyes, side-to-side;
　　nose, up-and-down.
　　　　Spring flowers!

Dawn

Dawnlight opening:
　　on the barley leaf tips
　　　　the hoarfrost of spring.

After Resigning His Position

A spring day—and:
　　in the garden, sparrows
　　　　bathing in the sand!

Summer Heat

Springtime, and it's "Hark!
　　They're singing!". . . . summer frogs
　　　　just bark!

Me | *wa* | *yoko-ni* | *hana* | *wa* | *tate* | *nari* | *haru-no* | *hana*
Eyes | as-for | horizontally | nose | as-for | vertical | it-is |
spring's | flowers

Akebono | *ya* | *mugi-no* | *ha-zue-no* | *haru-no-shimo*
Dawn | : | barley's | leaf-tips' | spring-hoarfrost

Haru-no-hi | *ya* | *niwa* | *ni* | *suzume-no* | *suna-abite*
Spring-day | : | garden | in | sparrows' | sand-bathing

Haru | *wa* | *naku* | *natsu-no-kawazu* | *wa* | *hoe-ni-keri*
Spring | as-for | sing | summer-frogs | as-for | bark

Coolness

How cool the breeze:
   the sky is filled with voices—
      pine and cedar trees.

The Open-Air Bath

There is no place
   to throw the used bath water.
      Insect cries!

The Weeping Willow

How strong a green
   are the strings of willow branches:
      the flowing of the stream!

The World Upside Down

A trout leaps high—
   below him, in the river bottom,
      clouds flow by.

Suzu-kaze | *ya* | *kokū* | *ni* | *michite* | *matsu-no-koe*
Cool-breeze | : | void-sky | in | filling | pine-tree-voices

Gyōzui-no | *sute-dokoro* | *nashi* | *mushi-no-koe*
Used-water's | throwing-place | there-is-not | insect-voices

Ara-ao-no | *yanagi-no* | *ito* | *ya* | *mizu-no* | *nagare*
Strong-green | willows' | strings | : | water's | flowing

Tobu | *ayu-no* | *soko* | *ni* | *kumo* | *yuku* | *nagare* | *kana*
Leaping | trout's | bottom | at | clouds | go | flowing | *kana*

"The Cuckoo Across the Moon"

Dark the night is, true,
  but to my ears a moonlit night,
    —cuckoo!

Green Fields

Green fields of grain:
  a skylark rises—over there,
    comes down again.

Another important figure of the period was Chiyo (1703–1775), the greatest of the women haiku composers. She was unquestionably a very fine poet, and it is difficult for foreigners to understand why her verse is not ranked more highly by the Japanese, some of whom go so far as to say that she knew nothing whatever about haiku. It has been claimed that this is because she is a woman, but one reason seems to be that her music is too pure; it can be utterly poignant, but it lacks overtones. In other words, most of her poems do not serve as starting points for trains of thought; they state one emotion clearly, but other associated emotions do not crowd into the reader's mind.

One European admirer of Chiyo has said bitterly

Yami-no-yo | *ga* | *mimi-ni* | *tsuki-no-yo* | *hototogisu*
Dark-night | but | ears-to | moon-night | cuckoo

The cuckoo and the moon have a traditional association, and the "cuckoo across the moon" is the subject of many paintings.

Ao-mugi | *ya* | *hibari* | *ga* | *agaru* | *are* | *sagaru*
Green-grain | : | skylark | [subj.] | rises | yonder | comes-down

that her poems are not hazy enough to be haiku, and there is enough truth in this to make it worth considering. What Chiyo's defender meant was that it is very easy to mistake haziness for profundity, and there are so-called haiku, produced by the hundred thousand, which are not profound at all, but merely foggy. This is true, and it is one of the dangers of the apparently easy haiku form. But of course it is not a valid criticism of real haiku.

Here it will be considered that both estimates of Chiyo are correct: that she was a true poet, but not a haiku master. Her finest poem is probably the one she wrote after the death of her little son. A fairly literal translation is:

> The dragonfly hunter—
>   today, what place has he
>   got to, I wonder. . . .

This has been beautifully rendered by Curtis Hidden Page as:

> I wonder in what fields today
> He chases dragonflies in play,
> My little boy—who ran away.

It is pure poignant emotion, and if it is "not haiku," it is simply in the sense that English is not Greek: they are different languages. Page's version has perhaps an added poignancy in the "ran away"—the feeling that the mother cannot bring herself to utter the word "died." But it does miss the effect of *made* in the original—the suggestion of "how far has he gone in his journey in the next world?"—a journey believed to be

Tombo-tsuri | *kyō* | *wa* | *doko* | *made* | *itta* | *yara*
Dragonfly-catcher | today | as-for | what-place | up-to | has-gone | ? | [I wonder]

very hard for children unless they had the protection of Jizō Bosatsu, their special guardian.

Chiyo's most often translated poem is:

> By morning glories
>> I have had my well-bucket captured—
>> and I borrow my water!

This is an attempt at being literal, though in the original the last line is a compound noun. The following paraphrase (by Clara M. Walsh) puts clearly what Chiyo only suggests:

> All round the rope a morning-glory clings;
> How can I break its beauty's dainty spell?
> I beg for water from a neighbor's well.

As a further example of why Chiyo's poems are not considered to be really haiku, compare the following (which may be called *Forgiveness*):

> To those who come
>> and break them, they give fragrance—
>> blossoms of the plum.

with one by Rosen (1654–1733):

> Blooms on the plum—
>> and repentance for anger at people
>> also has come.

Asagao | *ni* | *tsurube* | *torarete* | *morai* | *-mizu*
Morning-glories | by | well-bucket | being-captured | ask-for-and-get | water

Taoraruru | *hito* | *ni* | *kaoru* | *ya* | *ume-no-hana*
Breaking | person | to | are-fragrant | *ya* | plum-blossoms

Ume | *saite* | *hito-no* | *ikari-no* | *kui* | *mo* | *ari*
Plums | blooming | men-at | anger's | repentance | also | exists

The subjects are similar, and the poem attributed to
Chiyo is undoubtedly the more simple and charming.
But Rosen's has more overtones, and it makes use of
the internal comparison of ideas. It is not simply a
statement that with the coming of the blossoms that
presage the end of winter there comes also a feeling
of repentance for anger. The blossoms and the repentance are compared to each other, so that we get
the suggestion of repentance blossoming as the plums
do; of its beauty and sweetness; and of the melting
of the ice of anger and a promise of the warmth to
come. On the other hand, there is the thought that the
plum blossoms may be Nature's expression of repentance for her long coldness and her seeming anger
at humanity. Indeed, the poem will serve as a starting
point for many thoughts and emotions. The two poems
do give utterly different effects, and Rosen's is haiku.

Whether or not Chiyo wrote haiku is, however, perhaps a somewhat academic question. She certainly
wrote charming, if somewhat "feminine" verses, such
as:

> Had they no voice
>   the herons would be lost—
>   this morning's snow!

and

> Whatever we wear
>   we become beautiful—
>   moon-viewing!

Koe | naku-ba | sagi | ushinawamu | kesa-no | yuki
Voice | if-not | herons | would-be-lost | this-morning's |
snow

Nani-kite-mo | utsukushiu | naru | tsuki-mi | kana
Whatever-wearing | beautiful | became | moon-viewing |
kana

And I cannot resist adding one of my own special
favorites:

> Where the stream bed lies,
>   only there is darkness flowing:
>   fireflies!

The other authors whose haiku are given in the following pages belonged to various schools. But before
going on to them, at least one example should be
given of a quite popular type of haiku, in which the
effect is tried for by introducing objects utterly unpoetic in themselves. The one chosen for translation
here was composed by Fugyoku.

> The harvest moon:
>   and no dark place to empty
>   the ash-tray-spittoon.

A *haifuki* is used as both spittoon and ash tray, and
certainly is unpoetic enough. The point of the poem is
to contrast the glory of the moon with the pleasant
homely picture of several gentlemen of the old school
sitting around, smoking, talking, and enjoying it. It is
not meant to be funny.

Kawa | *bakari* | *yami* | *wa* | *nagarete* | *hotaru* | *kana*
River | only | darkness | as-for | flowing | fireflies | *kana*

Meigetsu | *ya* | *haifuki* | *suteru* | *kage* | *mo* | *nashi*
Bright-moon | : | ash tray | empty | shadow | even |
not-exist

Spring in My Hut

My hut in spring!
    True, there is nothing in it—
        there is Everything!

SODŌ (1641–1716)

The Passing of Spring

Spring—and already
    the yellow rose whitens;
        the lettuce tastes bitter.

SODŌ

Moon Magic

Leading me along,
    my shadow goes back home
        from looking at the moon.

SODŌ

Yado-no | *haru* | *nanimo* | *naki* | *koso* | *nanimo* | *are*
Hut's | spring | everything | is-not | indeed | everything | is

The use of a positive verb after *nanimo* is so unusual and striking that capitalizing "Everything" seems the only way to indicate the effect.

Haru | *mohaya* | *yama-buki* | *shiroku* | *chisha* | *nigashi*
Spring | already | yellow-rose | white | lettuce | is-bitter

Ware | *wo* | *tsurete* | *waga* | *kage* | *kaeru* | *tsukimi-kana*
Me | [acc.] | taking-along | my | shadow | returns-home | moon-viewing

In the Paddy Field

Women, rice-planting:
  all muddy, save for one thing—
    that's their chanting.

RAIZAN (1653–1716)

Springtime

Gathering, gathering—
  and then throwing them away:
    grasses in the spring.

RAIZAN

Autumn

Through the shutters it came,
  autumn's own shape: the warp
    of the candle flame.

RAIZAN

Sa-otome | *ya* | *yogorenu* | *mono* | *wa* | *uta* | *bakari*
Rice-field-women | : | not-soiled | thing | as-for | song |
only

Mushitte-wa | *mushitte-wa* | *sute* | *haru-no-kusa*
Plucking-up | plucking-up | throw-away | spring-grasses

Amado | *kosu* | *aki-no* | *sugata* | *ya* | *hi-no* | *kurui*
Wooden-shutter | pass-through | autumn's | shape | : |
flame's | derangement

If

I would pick from you,
   if it *were* a blossom spray—
      one trill, cuckoo!

KODŌ (d. 1738)

The Wild Geese Leave

Wild geese! I know
   that they did eat the barley;
      yet, when they go . . .

YASUI (1657–1743)

Coolness in Summer

In all this cool
   is the moon also sleeping?
      There, in the pool?

RYUSUI (1691–1758)

Hana | *naraba* | *hito* | *koe* | *oramu* | *hototogisu*
Flower | if-it-were | one | voicing | would-break-off |
cuckoo

Mugi | *kuishi* | *kari* | *to* | *omoedo* | *wakare* | *kana*
Barley | did-eat | wild-geese | thus | although-think |
parting | *kana*

Suzushisa | *ni* | *tsuki* | *mo* | *nemuru* | *ka* | *mizu-no* | *naka*
Coolness | in | moon | too | sleep | ? | water's | within

The Firefly Hunt

The lost child cries,
  and as he cries, he clutches
    at the fireflies.

RYUSUI

Watching

Above the veil
  of mist, from time to time
    there lifts a sail.

CAKOKU (early 18th cent.)

In Exile

In my old home, still
  my parents live.—The insect-cries
    are shrill. . . .

ANONYMOUS

Mayoi-go-no | *naku* | *naku* | *tsukamu* | *hotaru* | *kana*
Lost-child's | crying | crying | grasp-at | fireflies | *kana*

Kasumi | *yori* | *toki-doki* | *amaru* | *hokake-bune*
Mist | from | time-to-time | be-above | sail-boat

Furusato | *ni* | *fubo* | *ari* | *mushi-no* | *koe* | *takashi*
Old-village | in | parents | are | insect's | voices | are-high

Chapter VI

BUSON

In the second half of the eighteenth century the great figure in the haiku world was Taniguchi Buson (1715–83), who is regarded in Japan as second only to Bashō. He was almost equally famous as a painter, but curiously little is known about his life, and his personality has to be guessed at from his poems themselves. Japanese commentators think of Bashō and Buson as complementary to each other, and call them "the two pillars of haiku." They are certainly poles apart. Bashō was gentle, wise, loving, and mystic; Buson was brilliant and many-sided, not mystic in the least, but intensely clever and alive to impressions of the world around him. A foreign simile would be to liken Bashō to a pearl and Buson to a diamond. A Japanese would probably understand it better if one said that the difference between the two men was much the same as that between the great Sung landscapes and the brilliant paintings of the best of Ming.

Just because Buson was so many-sided, it is impossible to take any of his poems as typical. But some idea of his quality may be obtained from comparing pairs of his poems on the same subject. On the subject of plum blossoms, for instance:

> From the plum-tree bloom
>   does the fragrancy float upward?
>   There's a halo round the moon!

is simply a charming fantasy, and a pleasing picture, with nothing more intended, while,

> The plum trees bloom—
>   and pleasure women buy new sashes
>   in a brothel room.

with its reference to *yūjo*, then primarily "high-class" indentured women of brothel districts like the Yoshi-wara, which they were practically never allowed to leave, gains added poignancy from being such a color-ful scene.

The next pair has to do with flowers of the rape, a plant widely cultivated for the oil from its seeds, and whose brilliant yellow blossoms make a sharp contrast with the deep green of its leaves. The first:

> Yellow rape in bloom;
>   in the west there is the sun—
>   in the east, the moon.

Ume-ga-ka-no | tachi-noborite | ya | tsuki-no | kasa
Plum's-fragrance's | climbing-upward | ? | moon's | halo

Ume | saite | obi-kau | heya-no | yūjo | kana
Plums | blooming | sashes-buying | room's | courtesans | kana

Na-no-hana | ya | tsuki | wa | higashi-ni | hi | wa | nishi-ni
Rape-flowers | : | moon | [as-for] | east-in | sun | [as-for] | west-in

gives the picture of an enormous field without mentioning its size. No mood is suggested; the reader can supply his own. In the second, the poet's mood of temporary indecision is very delicately suggested by the pause which comes naturally after *wa*. I have tried to render it by using a dash after "and":

> Yellow rape in bloom:
>> I come up to the priest's house, and—
>>> not stopping in, pass on.

On the subject of spring rain, which, in contradistinction to the May-June rain, is thought of primarily as being very soft and gentle, Buson wrote some thirty haiku, of which I can here give only four. Of the thirty, the most famous one is probably:

> Springtime rain: together,
>> intent upon their talking, go
>>> straw-raincoat and umbrella.

It is hardly necessary to state that the raincoat would be worn by a man, and the umbrella used by a girl. The second is in very formal, rather old-fashioned language.

> The rain of spring:
>> in the carriage that we share,
>>> my dear one's whispering.

Na-no-hana | *ya* | *hōshi-ga* | *yado* | *wa* | *towade* | *sugi*
Rape-flowers | : | priest's | house | [as-for] | not-calling-at | pass-on

Harusame | *ya* | *monogatari-yuku* | *mino* | *to* | *kasa*
Spring-rain | : | conversing-go | raincoat | and | umbrella

Harusame | *ya* | *dō-sha-no* | *kimi-no* | *sasamegoto*
Spring-rain | : | same-vehicle's | dear-one's | whispering

The formality of the wording suggests that the two people are probably a Court nobleman and his lady. The carriage would therefore naturally be visualized as one of the covered oxcarts, with a single axle and two enormous black lacquered wheels, which had been used by the nobility for many centuries. The third is a simple description of the rain, in language which is almost that of a child:

> Spring rain: and as yet
> the little froglets' bellies
> haven't got wet.

The fourth is utterly Buson; it has its effect, but I cannot describe it:

> As the spring rains fall,
> soaking in them, on the roof,
> is a child's rag ball.

Some of Buson's poems suggest the darker side of things, as does this one about mandarin ducks, which in Japan are symbols of married happiness:

> A mandarin pair!
> But the pond is old, and its weasel
> is watching there.

Others are frankly *vers de société*, and none the worse for that, although to appreciate them properly

Harusame | *ya* | *kawazu-no* | *hara-no* | *mada* | *nurezu*
Spring-rain | : | frog's | bellies' | as-yet | not-get-wet

Harusame | *ni* | *nuretsutsu* | *yane-no* | *te-mari* | *kana*
Spring-rain | in | being-soaked | roof's | hand-ball | *kana*

Oshidori | *ya* | *itachi-no* | *nozoku* | *ike* | *furushi*
Mandarin-ducks | : | weasel's | peep | pond | is-old

one naturally has to have at least some knowledge of
the customs of old-time Japanese society. Thus the
following poem, apparently addressed by a young
gentleman to a young lady of the Court:

> No poem you send
> in answer——Oh, young lady!
> Springtime nears its end!

loses much of its point unless one realizes that the
exchange of poems, even love poems, was regarded as
a social accomplishment rather than anything more
serious; and also that *ao*, which here means "young,"
has a basic meaning of "green," and can be interpreted
in the exact sense of modern English slang. The last
line can be taken either as an expression of regret or
as an intimation that the lady had better gather rose-
buds while she may.

These few examples do not even begin to cover the
range of Buson's variety, but they do at least show the
complete difference between him and Bashō. His
poems often have a depth of their own, but it is very
definitely not the same kind of depth. Even when, as
sometimes happens, deep philosophic meanings can
be read into some of Buson's haiku, such interpreta-
tions are to be regarded with grave suspicion. It is
credibly reported that a serious-minded foreign stu-
dent once thought he had found a profound esoteric
philosophy (something about the oneness of terror
and beauty) in one of Buson's rare haiku on religious
subjects—the one about Emma Ō, the Lord of Hell.
The haiku is:

Hen-ka | *naki* | *ao-nyōbo* | *yo* | *kure-no* | *haru*
Answer-poem | not | young-court-lady | ! | ending | spring

> Emma Ō's mouth! See!
>   From which he is about to spit
>   a peony!

But after he had come to Japan and seen the many statues depicting the great round crimson mouth of the god, even he was forced to change his opinion. Incidentally, there has been a disagreement among Japanese haiku experts as to whether Buson intended to describe the god's mouth by comparing it to a red peony, or vice-versa. Being Buson, he might well have meant either—or possibly both.

Many of Buson's poems do convey a feeling of the wonder and mystery of nature, but the feeling usually depends so much on overtones that it is likely to be lost in translation. This is true even of haiku that can be translated fairly literally, such as:

> The cherry-bloom has gone—
>   a temple, in among the trees,
>   is what it has become.

In the original the *to naru* suggests that the temple, which can now be seen through the denuded branches, is only one aspect of the cherry bloom, and a temporary one at that.* In this particular poem there is perhaps a certain Buddhist influence, but to me it seems that Buson's approach is poetic rather than religious.

---

* Compare with the poem on p. 106, where the *ni naru* suggests a change that is complete and permanent.

Emma Ō | *no* | *kuchi* | *ya* | *botan* | *wo* | *hakan-to-su*
Emma Ō | 's | mouth | : | peony | [acc.] | is-about-to-spit

Hana | *chirite* | *ko-no-ma-no* | *tera* | *to* | *nari-ni-keri*
Bloom(s) | falling | tree-interval | temple | [that] | has-become *keri*

Actually very little is known of Buson's philosophy, and outside of his poetry and painting he apparently never did formulate one. We do know that he must have enormously enjoyed the ever-changing aspects of the passing world, though more as an observer than by in any way identifying himself with them. He did, however, have his own theories of how nature should be enjoyed, and one of his most famous haiku:

> To cherry blooms I come,
>   and under the blossoms go to sleep—
>   no duties to be done!

is an effective plea against the over-formalization of the appreciation of nature which was—and is—one of the dangers of Japanese aestheticism. Here, of course, he is indicating that enjoyment of leisure does not require "viewing" the cherry blossoms and writing poems about them.

Buson always seems to be at least as much interested in the manner as in the matter of his poems. He had an absolute mastery of technique, and an exuberant joy in using it that is a constant delight to the reader. This mastery of technique led him to use tone color and onomatopoeia to an extent far beyond that of any previous haiku poet, and unfortunately this makes some of his best haiku practically untranslatable. For instance:

Hana-ni | *kite* | *hana-ni* | *inemuru* | *itoma* | *kana*
Blossoms-to | coming | blossoms-at | go-to-sleep | leisure-time | *kana*

By day, "Day go away!"
　　by night, "Night turn to light!"—that's what
　　　the croaking frogs say.

is one of the strongly onomatopoeic haiku. The reader
is recommended to try saying the Japanese original
out loud rapidly, remembering that the vowels have
almost the same sound as in Italian, and that they are
all pronounced, except for a final "u," which is usually
elided. If the reader does as suggested he will certainly sound like a frog.

One of his finest—and most untranslatable—haiku is:

The springtime sea:
　　all day long up-and-down,
　　　up-and-down gently.

This translation is an attempt to keep some of the
rhythm of the original, but there is something about
the sound of *hinemos' notari notari kana* that makes
one want to go on repeating it until one is almost
drugged.

There is one particular instance of matching sound
to sense, in which the resulting form is so peculiar
that there is some doubt as to whether or not it can
be considered haiku at all:

*Hi | wa | hi | kure | yo | yo | wa | yo | ake | yo | to |
naku-kawazu*

Day | as-for | day | darken | ! | Night | as-for | night |
lighten | ! | thus | croaking-frogs

Haru-no-umi | hinemosu | notari | notari | kana
Spring-sea | all-day-long | undulating | undulating | *kana*

As the moon-brilliance westward makes its
    crossing, so
cherry-blossom shadows eastward
    slowly go.

The original, instead of having the conventional syllable count of 5, 7, 5, has one of 11, 8, 5; it also has the
kind of parallelism that one expects in a Chinese
couplet. The long first line does give an effect of a
slow passage of time, and there is a quite interesting
contrast of the very "Chinese" *gekkō* with the very
Japanese *hana-kage*, but Buson does not seem to have
been wholly satisfied with the result, as he apparently
never tried a similar experiment again. Nevertheless
this poem has often been cited, especially by later
poets, as proof that a poem may vary very greatly from
the standard 5, 7, 5 form and still be haiku.

On the other hand, Buson often carried the principle of economy of words to its ultimate extent. Take
the following:

Comes to donate
    trout, does not enter, passes on—
        midnight gate.

In an elementary Japanese book on the study of haiku
its author states that this might well be unintelligible
to anyone not trained in haiku reading, and goes on
to explain at some length:

Gekkō | *nishi-ni* | *watareba*
Moon-brilliance | west-to | when-crosses
hana-kage | *higashi-ni* | *ayumu* | *kana*
blossom-shadows | east-to | walk-slowly | *kana*

Ayu | *kurete* | *yorade* | *sugi-yuku* | *yowa-no-mon*
Trout | giving | not-visiting | passes-on | midnight-gate

"We have first a voice at midnight at the entrance-gate of some person's house; then that person getting up and finding that it comes from some friend of his who had obtained some trout, either by catching them that night or otherwise, and who therefore offers to share with him; finally, although the visitor has been invited to come in, he refuses on account of the late hour or for some such reason, and continues on his way." He adds that "in accordance with the haiku conventions" the reader must supply words indicating that somebody performed the action, that it was performed at the gate, etc., as "the omission of words is to be expected in haiku."

After one gets the picture, the final feeling is one of friendliness and companionship. But the cleverness in the intentional obscurity is that it duplicates the feelings of the master of the house; as the meaning becomes clearer, gradually the darkness goes, and we are sorry to part with our friend when he finally leaves us standing at the midnight gate.

Buson uses the same technique, often very effectively, in other haiku designed to tell a story:

"Night's lodging!"—so
     calls out, and throws his sword down—
          wind-blown snow!

The original is even terser, as it has no personal pronouns at all, and the word *to* (thus) suggests calling out without actually saying it. Nevertheless the pic-

Yado-kase | *to* | *katana* | *nage-dasu* | *fubuki* | *kana*
Give-lodging | thus | sword | throws-down | blown-snow | *kana*

ture is quite clear to anyone who knows "the haiku conventions"—that of an exhausted fugitive entering unexpectedly. It does not matter whether it is an inn or a farmhouse, or whether the man who storms in sword in hand is a robber or a samurai—though, as Blyth points out, it may make a better picture to consider him a samurai. Here the "wind-blown snow" performs three functions: it sets the seasonal background; it enters with the unknown man through the door he must have opened; and it is compared to him, and he to it.

In addition to being a poet, Buson was also a painter. Hence his visual sense was highly developed, and it will already have been noticed that the settings of many of his haiku are quite charming pictures in themselves. Unfortunately, it is often difficult for foreigners to get their full effect—and especially so for foreigners who have not lived in Japan. For example, in the following haiku the first word is *ikada*, which is commonly translated as "raft." But to a Japanese the word brings up the idea of a loosely joined log float, which is usually sent down the rivers in spring when the water is high. And he will also get a vision of the normal Japanese river, rather small from our point of view, rocky, and winding down between sharply rising hills. Thus the background of the picture is prepared. The *mino*, which is marked as the important word by the *ya* that follows it, is peculiarly Japanese. It is a sort of raincoat made of reeds or rice straw, and consists of the *mino* proper, which is worn around the shoulders like a cape, and of the *koshi-mino*, which is often added to it wrapped around the body down to about the knees. Wide mushroom-shaped straw hats are nearly always worn along with this costume. We must know all this before we can get the picture:

> Raftsmen on their floats;
>> their straw capes—see them!—in the storm,
>> cherry-blossom coats.

The last part of the poem shows us the storm-wind sweeping through the cherry trees—common to all Japan—and filling the air with flying petals, many of which stick to the wet *mino* of the raftsmen and make their robes more gorgeous than any nishiki brocades.

In the following example it is a necessary prerequisite to have at least some knowledge of Japanese painting:

> Into a line they wheel,
>> the wild geese; at the foothills,
>> the moon is put for seal.

The word *gyō*, here translated as "line," usually refers to a line or short passage of writing, which in normal Japanese would be perpendicular, or nearly so, and which, when put in a painting, would usually be in the upper part. This shows that the geese are not flying horizontally but have turned and are coming downward, though still above the foothills and the moon. It also sets the season as autumn, when the wild geese come into Japan from the North, to spend the winter. The subject is a favorite one for artists, and the picture would be easily visualized by almost any Japanese, complete with foothills and the mountain or mountains they imply. Buson, however, has suggested the idea of a line of writing, which in Japan is

Ikada-shi-no | mino | ya | arashi-no | hana-goromo
Raftsmen's | straw coats | : | storm's | blossom-robes

Ichi gyō no | kari | ya | hayama-ni | tsuki | wo | in-su
One-line's | wild-geese | : | foothills-at | moon | [acc.] | make-seal

often used as almost the equivalent of a painting, so that the scene may be visualized in more than one way. In any case, however, the moon seal is where it belongs, near the bottom of the long hanging scroll. After one gets the picture is time enough to notice that Buson has not said clearly who it is that uses the moon for seal. That question is left for the reader to go to bed with.

As a complete contrast to the "picture" type, one may take the following, a haiku from which I have received considerable pleasure, in spite of, or perhaps because of, the fact that the more one thinks about it the less clear the picture becomes. It is, as accurately as I can give it:

> A mountain pheasant,
> > treading on its tail, the springtime's
> > setting sun.

I am glad to say that Japanese experts seem to share both my pleasure and my perplexity. The poem has been much discussed, but no agreement has been reached even as to who does the treading, the sun or the bird itself—it depends on how one groups the words—or as to just how either feat would be accomplished. (Grammatically, it might even be the spring that does it, but this seems unlikely.) The only solid facts we have are that the pheasant is highly colored, and that its tail is very long. There are strong suggestions of an equally highly colored sunset, and of at least one long ray from it, which may, or may not, strike the pheasant's tail. After that, things run into each other and get confused. This is certainly not a

Yama-dori-no | *o* | *wo* | *fumu* | *haru no* | *iri-hi* | *kana*
Mountain-pheasant's | tail | [acc.] | treading | spring's | setting-sun | *kana*

normal haiku, but I cannot help having the feeling that Buson, who was both an experimenter and a master craftsman, may perhaps have achieved exactly the effect that he intended.

Obviously it is impossible to give for every poem such long explanations as have been given for the last few. And it would be wrong to do so even if it were possible, for haiku were not written to be weighed down with commentary. I cannot, however, resist adding one that is a favorite of mine, probably because I had felt the mood before reading the poem. It has to do with the "slow days" at the beginning of the year, when nothing seems to change, and today is just like yesterday.

> The days are slow:
>   there are echoings one hears
>   in a corner of Kyō.

Kyō (Kyoto) was the capital of the Emperors for over a thousand years, and one cannot live there even today without a feeling that the past is all around one. In Buson's time, with the Emperor still there, the feeling must have been even stronger.

The comparatively few poems that follow—Buson wrote well over two thousand—require little comment, except that poems on the "short nights" usually refer to the end of the short nights of early summer. Also, the two poems mentioning screens may possibly have some sort of relationship. The one about "Summer Garments" (page 112) is said to be a lament at the death of a certain lady of the Court. In the original form the screens were silver, instead of gold, as is the one in the poem about the short night (page 108).

Osoki | hi | ya | kodama | kikoyuru | Kyō-no | sumi
Slow | days | : | echoes | get-heard | capital's | corner

This at least tends to support the opinion that the second poem contains somewhat pornographic suggestions, which certainly can be found in a considerable number of Buson's haiku. Those who are interested in technique may find it interesting to compare Buson's "objective" treatment of the departure of the wild geese (page 105) with Yasui's "subjective" treatment of the same subject (page 88).

Spring Scene

On the temple bell
  has settled, and is fast asleep,
    a butterfly.

The Sound

Here . . . there . . .
  the sound of waterfalls is heard—
    young leaves, everywhere.

Tsurigane-ni | *tomarite* | *nemuru* | *kochō* | *kana*
Temple-bell-on | settling | sleep | butterfly | *kana*

Ochi-kochi-no | *take-no* | *oto* | *kiku* | *waka-ba* | *kana*
Here-and-there | waterfall's | sound | hear | young-leaves | *kana*

The Unseen Road

Warehouses in a row—
  behind them is a road, where swallows
    come and go.

Regret at Parting

Yesterday a flight;
  today a flight; the wild geese
    are not here tonight!

Symphony in White

Blossoms on the pear—
  and a woman in the moonlight
    reads a letter there.

Kura | *narabu* | *ura* | *wa* | *tsubame-no* | *kayoi* | *michi*
Warehouses | aligned | back | as-for | swallows' |
come-and-go | road

Kino | *ini* | *kyō* | *ini* | *kari-no* | *naki* | *yo* | *kana*
Yesterday | going | today | going | wild-geese's | not-be |
night | *kana*

Nashi-no | *hana* | *tsuki* | *ni* | *fumi-yomu* | *onna* | *ari*
Pear's | blossoms | moon | by | letter-reading | woman |
there-is

Cherry Petals

Scattered petals lie
   on rice-seedling waters:
      bright is the starlit sky.

Fallen Splendor

The scattering bloom—
   does it turn into torn wastepaper?
      A bamboo broom!

Spring's Departure

Departing spring:
   with belated cherry blossoms
      shilly-shallying.

Sakura | *chiru* | *nawa-shiro* | *mizu* | *ya* | *hoshi-zuki* | *yo*
Cherries | scatter | rice-seedling | water | : | star-moon |
night

Chiru | *hana-no* | *hōgu* | *ni* | *naru* | *ya* | *take-bōki*
Falling | blossoms' | trash | into | turning | ? |
bamboo-broom

Garden brooms were usually very roughly made of bamboo
twigs.

Yuku-haru | *ya* | *shun-jun* | *to* | *shite* | *oso-zakura*
Going-spring | : | shilly-shally | thus | doing | late-cherries

The Ōi River in Flood

With all the rains of May
    in the Ōi, I have crossed it!
        Pretty clever—eh?

The Lover

What utter delight
    to the eye—my dearest one's fan,
        so perfectly white!

The Short Night (I)

Night that ends so soon:
    in the ford there still remains
        one sliver of the moon.

Samidare-no | *Ōi* | *koshitaru* | *kashikosa* | *yo*
May-rain's | Ōi | have-crossed | cleverness | !

Me | *ni* | *ureshi* | *koi-gimi-no* | *sen* | *ma-shiro* | *nari*
Eye | to | gives-joy | loved-one's | fan | pure-white | it-is

  Fine fans were usually painted, quite often by famous
artists.

Mijika | *yo* | *ya* | *asase-ni* | *nokoru* | *tsuki* | *ip-pen*
Short | night | : | shallows-in | remaining | moon | one-part

The Short Night (II)

Short the night has been:
    close beside my pillow
        stands a silver screen.

The Short Night (III)

The short night is through:
    on the hairy caterpillar,
        little beads of dew.

Spring Breeze

These morning airs—
    one can see them stirring
        caterpillar hairs!

Mijika | *yo* | *ya* | *makura* | *ni* | *chikaki* | *gin-byōbu*
Short | night | : | pillow | to | near | silver-screen

Mijika | *yo* | *ya* | *kemushi-no* | *ue* | *ni* | *tsuyu-no-tama*
Short | night | : | hairy-caterpillar's | top | on | dew-beads

Asa-kaze-no | *ka* | *wo* | *fuki-miyuru* | *kemushi* | *kana*
Morning-breeze's | hairs | [acc.] | blowing-is-seen |
caterpillar | *kana*

The Portent

There is no stir,
   not even one leaf; awesome
      is the summer grove.

Flowering Thorn

Flowering thorn—
   how like the roads about the place
      where I was born!

The Red Peony

It falls, the peony—
   and upon each other lie
      petals, two or three.

Ugoku | *ha* | *mo* | *naku* | *osoroshiki* | *natsu-kodachi*
Moving | leaf | even | not-exist | frightening |
summer-grove

Hana-ibara | *kokyō-no* | *michi* | *ni* | *nitaru* | *kana*
Flower-thorn | old-home's | roads | to | are-similar | *kana*

Botan | *chirite* | *uchi-kasanarinu* | *ni-san-pen*
Peony | scattering | have-piled-up | two-three-petals

Creeping Shadows

A deer along with it,
  the mountain's shadow at the temple gate—
    the setting sun.

Autumn Ripples

Far away the snipe go—
  on the water are ripples,
    made cleaning the hoe.

The Whale

A whale!
  Down it goes, and more and more
    up goes its tail!

Shika | *nagara* | *yama-kage* | *mon* | *ni* | *iri-hi* | *kana*
Deer | along | mountain-shadow | gate | at | setting-sun | *kana*

Shigi | *tōku* | *kuwa* | *susugu* | *mizu-no* | *uneri* | *kana*
Snipe | afar | hoe | wash | water's | undulation | *kana*

Kujira | *ochite* | *iyo-iyo* | *takaki* | *o-age* | *kana*
Whale | going-down | more-and-more | high | tail-up | *kana*

Haze

Morning haze:
    as in a painting of a dream,
      men go their ways.

Autumn Leaves

To Lord Toba's Hall
    five or six horsemen hurry hard—
      a storm-wind of the fall!

Parting

For me who go,
    for you who stay—
      two autumns.

Asa-giri | ya | e | ni | kaku | yume-no | hito-dōri
Morning-haze | : | picture | in | paint | dream's |
people-passing

Toba-dono | e | go-rok-ki | isogu | nowaki | kana
Toba-Hall | toward | five-six-riders | hasten |
autumn-storm | *kana*

Toba Tennō ruled in the twelfth century, most of the
time after having technically abdicated, at a period when
Japan was in a tumult of civil war.

Yuku | ware | ni | todomaru | nare | ni | aki | futatsu
Going | I | for | staying | you | for | autumns | two

Summer Garments

Upon the golden screens
are summer garments—whose?
The autumn wind . . .

The Way of Things

If a west wind blows,
they pile up in the east—
the fallen leaves.

Borrowed Armor

Borrowed armor, old,
getting fitted to my body—
oh, it's cold!

Kin-byō-no | *usu-mono* | *wa* | *tare* | *ka* | *aki-no-kaze*
Gold-screen's | thin-garments | as-for | who | ? |
autumn-wind

The *Tagasode* ("Whose Clothes") design, usually
painted on a background of gold foil, was a very common
decorative motif for pairs of large folding screens. As I see
it Buson is looking at one of these, but remembering real
garments once hung on a plain screen. The poem is said
to be a lament for a dead lady.

Nishi | *fukaba* | *higashi* | *ni* | *tamaru* | *ochi-ba* | *kana*
West | if-blow | east | in | heap-up | fallen-leaves | *kana*

Kari | *yoroi* | *ware-ni* | *najimaru* | *samusa* | *kana*
Borrowed | armor | me-to | get-fitted | cold | *kana*

The Sudden Chillness

The piercing chill I feel:
  my dead wife's comb, in our bedroom,
    under my heel . . .

Mi-ni-shimu | *ya* | *bō-sai-no* | *kushi* | *neya* | *ni* | *fumu*
Body-into-pierce | : | dead-wife's | comb | bedroom | in |
tread-on

Chapter VII

BUSON'S CONTEMPORARIES

THERE were a number of excellent haiku composers more or less contemporary with Buson, but it is not possible to consider them here at any length or to give more than a few of their haiku. Many of these are well known, and at least one has been adopted by common speech as part of a proverb. It is one by Ryōta, who was slightly younger than Buson—not his pupil, but a worthy scion of Bashō's school. He might be considered a poetical great-grandson, as his master had studied under Bashō's pupil Ransetsu.

> Oh, the wide world's ways!
>   Cherry blossoms left unwatched
>   even for three days!

It is used with two meanings, one being that the cherry blossoms have fallen, and the other that they

Yo-no-naka | wa | mik-ka | minu | ma | ni | sakura | kana
The-world | as-for | three-day | see-not | interval | in |
cherries | kana

have come out in all their glory. Given the second sense, it has become almost a cliché to use about the children of friends one may not have seen for some time. And this seems really the correct interpretation, for tradition has it that the poem was composed after the poet had stayed quietly at home for some days, and then one morning was disturbed by exuberant picnic parties going to see the cherry blossoms. Incidentally, the pleasant alliteration of *mikka minu ma ni* may well have had something to do with its popularity.

Taigi (d. 1771) and Kito (1740–88) were probably Buson's best pupils. For one of Taigi's poems, which I do not want to omit, I must give an explanation. The bird I have called a "fish hawk" is really a Siberian black kite, which flies higher than our osprey, but I wished to suggest the circular flight of the hawks with which most foreigners are familiar.

> Four miles round they go—
>   fish hawks, too, come out and dance
>   when the tide is low.

The effect of *mo* (too; also; even) is to make a comparison of the birds' circular "dance" with the dances at village festivals, where the participants form concentric circles, each of which moves as a unit. Incidentally, these dances last for many hours, and individuals fall out as they get exhausted, until only one circle is left, and this gets smaller and smaller until, theoretically—though not actually, in normal

Ni | ri | hodo | wa | tobi | mo | dete | mau | shio-hi | kana
Two | "ri" | extent-up-to | as-for | kites | also | coming-out | dance | low-tide | *kana*

practice—only one person is left. One has to know this
before he can get the full pleasure out of Buson's:

> On people, four or five
> the moon begins to set—
> the circle-dance!

Buson does not make the comparison explicitly, as
Taigi does, but to me the picture is a charming one,
leaving unresolved the question as to whether or not
the moon will be left as the last one, pursuing its own
"circle-dance."

There is another poem, by the nun Sogetsu (d.
1804), which in a way completes the trilogy. It has to
be paraphrased, as it starts in with *Bon-odori ato wa*,
which is literally "as for the afterward of the Bon-
dance," and one cannot expect foreigners to know that
o-bon is the festival for the dead, celebrated throughout Japan in mid-July, and more or less corresponding
to the Christian "Feast of All Souls." I hope that at
least some of the effect can be gotten from the paraphrase:

> The sound of dancing dies;
> wind among the pine trees,
> insect-cries.

There is one other well-known poem, which I hate to
burden with comment, but for which many people
will need an explanation:

Shi-go-nin | *ni* | *tsuki* | *ochi-kakaru* | *odori* | *kana*
Four-five-people | on | **moon** | begins-setting | dance | *kana*

Bon-odori | *ato* | *wa* | *matsu-kaza* | *mushi-no* | *koe*
Bon-dance | afterward | as-for | pine-tree-wind | insects' |
voices

> Melons! Till last year
> I scolded him about them—
> my offering here!

The verb *tamukeru* (offer) brings up the picture of the household shrine, at which offerings of flowers and fruit would be made to the spirits of the dead. The scolding about melons suggests a small boy who, like most small boys, was over-fond of them even when they were not ripe. It is to his spirit that the melons are offered. The poem was written by Ōemaru (1722–1805), who is affectionately remembered, not only for his own poetry, but also for the encouragement he gave in his old age to the young poet Issa, who is the subject of the next chapter.

The haiku by the poetess Seifu (d. 1814)

> Now this year goes away:
> I've no parents left, from whom
> to hide the gray.

which refers to the poem by Etsujin (p. 62) is particularly interesting as showing the influence of Bashō's pupils even after a hundred years had passed.

I cannot resist adding a somewhat freely translated anonymous poem, said to have been composed by a prisoner on the scaffold a moment before he was decapitated:

Kyō-nen | *made* | *shikatta* | *uri* | *wo* | *tamuke-keri*
Last-year | up-to | scolded-about | melons | [acc.] | offered-*keri*

Yuku-toshi | *ya* | *shiraga* | *wo* | *kakusu* | *oya* | *mo* | *nashi*
Departing-year | : | white-hairs | [acc.] | hide-from | parents | even | are-not

As for the end—
    that I'll hear in the next world,
        cuckoo, my friend.

It may or may not be a true story—or even actually of
the period—but it is a touching illustration of the re-
gard given both to haiku and to the song of "the bird
of the other world."

Spring

They have the guise
    of being married just today—
        those two butterflies.

RYŌTA (1718–87)

The Visitor

All the rains of June:
    and one evening, secretly,
        through the pines, the moon.

RYŌTA

Sono | ato | wa | meido | de | kikan | hototogisu
It's | afterward | as-for | next-world | in | will-hear | cuckoo

Ichi-nichi-no | tsuma | to | mie-keri | chō | futatsu
One-day's | spouses | thus | seem-keri | butterflies | two

Samidare | ya | aru | yo | hisokani | matsu-no | tsuki
June-rains | : | certain | night | secretly | pine-trees' |
moon

Communion

From them no words come:
  the guest, the host, the white
    chrysanthemum.

RYŌTA

Autumn Night

That there is only one
  is unbelievable tonight.
    This harvest moon!

RYŌTA

Harvest Moon

So brilliant a moonshine:
  if ever I am born again—
    a hilltop pine!

RYŌTA

Mono-iwazu | *kyaku* | *to* | *teishu* | *to* | *shira-giku* | *to*
Not-saying-anything | guest | [and] | host | [and] |
white-chrysanthemum | [and]

Hitotsu | *to* | *wa* | *omowanu* | *yo* | *nari* | *hyo-no-tsuki*
One | thus | as-for | unthinkable | night | it-is |
harvest-moon

Mei-getsu | *ya* | *umare-kawaraba* | *mine-no-matsu*
Bright-moon | : | if-born-again | hilltop-pine

Winter Evening

At the candle's light
I look, and yes—there is a wind.
The snow tonight . . .

RYŌTA

In My Host's Garden

"Don't break it!" he said,
then broke off and gave me
a branch of his plum.

TAIGI (d. 1771)

Night Scene

The bridge is down
and people stand upon the bank.
The summer moon . . .

TAIGI

Tomoshi-bi | *mireba* | *kaze* | *ari* | *yoru-no-yuki*
Light's flame | when-look | wind | there-is | evening-snow

Na | *ori* | *so* | *to* | *orite* | *kure-keri* | *sono-no* | *ume*
Don't | break | ! | thus | breaking | gave [me] | garden's |
plum

Hashi | *ochite* | *hito* | *kishi* | *ni* | *ari* | *natsu-no* | *tsuki*
Bridge | falling | people | bank | on | are | summer's | moon

Loneliness

A flitting firefly!
"Look! Look there!" I start to call—
    but there is no one by.

TAIGI

Haze

Evening haze:
    when memories come, how distant
    are the bygone days.

KITŌ (1740–88) Buson pupil

Marvels

"Marvelous!" I say,
    as I watch, now this, now that—
    and springtime goes away.

KITŌ

Tobu | hotaru | are | to | iwan-mo | hitori | kana
Flying | firefly | there | thus | although-would-say | alone |
kana

Yu-gasumi | omoeba | hedatsu | mukashi | kana
Evening-haze | when-think | be-far-off | old-time | kana

Mezurashi | to | miru-mono-goto-ni | haru | ya | yuku
Wonderful | thus | see-thing-each-at | spring | [subj.] |
goes

Regret for Spring's Passing

Regret for spring's passing—
    year after year, and yet
        never the same.

GEKKYŌ (d. 1824)

At an Ancient Temple

Tarnished is the gold—
    with young leaves round us, we look back
        to days of old.

CHORA (1729–81)

The Storm

A storm-wind blows—
    out from among the grasses
        the full moon grows.

CHORA

Haru | oshimu | kokoro | nen-nen | ni-zari-keri
Spring | regretting | feeling | year-year | not-the-same-keri

Kogane | sabite | waka-ba | ni | shinobu | mukashi | kana
Yellow-gold | tarnishing | young-leaves | in | look-back |
past | kana

Arashi | fuku | kusa-no | naka | yori | kyō-no-tsuki
Tempest | blow | grasses' | midst | from | today's-moon

Enjoyment

Look, and it starts misting;
    just don't look, and it clears—
        when gazing at the moon.

CHORA

The Road Block

Get out of my road
    and allow me to plant these
        bamboos, Mr. Toad!

CHORA

The Flower-Viewing

Women, children, men:
    into cherry bloom they push—
        from bloom come out again.

CHORA

Mireba | *kumori* | *minuba* | *hare-yuku* | *tsuki-mi* | *kana*
When-look | haze | if-not-look | clear-up | moon-viewing |
kana

Soko | *noite* | *take-ue-sase* | *yo* | *hiki-gaeru*
That-place | leaving | allow-bamboo-planting | ! | toad

Morobito | *ya* | *hana* | *wo* | *wake-iri* | *hana* | *wo* | *izu*
Everybody | : | blossoms | [acc.] | spreading-go-in |
blossoms | [acc.] | come-out-of

The End of Autumn

Frost! You may fall!
  After chrysanthemums there are
    no flowers at all!

ŌEMARU (1722–1805)

Spring Grove

The grove in spring:
  even the birds that prey on birds
    are slumbering.

RANKŌ (1726–99)

Withered Reeds

Day after day
  the withered reeds break off
    and drift away.

RANKŌ

Oke | ya | shimo | kiku | yori | nochi | wa | hana | mo | nashi

Leave | ! | frost | chrysanthemums | from | after | as-for | flowers | even | are-not

Haru-no-mori | tori | toru | tori | mo | neburi-keri

Spring-grove | birds | catch | birds | even | are-gone-to-sleep

Kare-ashi-no | hi | ni | hi | ni | orete | nageri-keri

Withered-reeds' | day | in | day | in | breaking | flow-*keri*

Summer Night

Summer night:
from cloud to cloud the moon
is swift in flight.

RANKŌ

Autumn

The falling leaves
fall and pile up; the rain
beats on the rain.

GYŌDAI (1732–93)

The Watchers

The whole spring night
guardians of the fields drive off
each wild-goose flight.

GYŌDAI

Natsu-no | *yo* | *ya* | *kumo* | *yori* | *kumo* | *ni* | *tsuki* | *hashiru*
Summer's | night | : | cloud | from | cloud | to | moon | runs

Ochiba | *ochi* | *kasanarite* | *ame* | *ame* | *wo* | *utsu*
Falling-leaves | fall | piling-up | rain | rain | [acc.] | beats

Haru-no-yo | *wo* | *kari* | *oi-akasu* | *no-mori* | *kana*
Spring-night | [acc.] | wild-geese | drive-away | field-guards | *kana*

"Setsugekka"
(*Snow, Moon, and Flowers*)

The moon, the snow,
　　and now besides—through mist,
　　　the morning glow!

MICHIHIKO (d. 1818)

Snow

Such a lot of snow
　　that to do snow-viewing
　　　there's no place to go!

ANON. (late 18th cent.)

At the Year's End

The old year goes away:
　　and the things it takes with it,
　　　what and what are they?

SŌIN (late 18th cent.)

Tsuki | yuki-no | hoka-ni | kasumi-no | asa-borake
Moon | snow's | besides | mist's | dawn-breaking

Ō-yuki | ya | yuki | wo | mi-ni | yuku | tokoro | nashi
Big-snow | : | snow | [acc.] | to-see | go | place | is-not

Yuku-toshi | ya | tsuredatsu | mono | wa | nani | to | nani
Going-year | : | take-along-with | things | as-for | what |
and | what

The Courtesan's Prayer

If of love I die,
   then above my grave mound,
      cuckoo—come and cry!

OSHU (late 18th cent., a courtesan)

The Skylark

A song alone
   comes down—and of the skylark
      the last trace is gone.

AMPŪ (late 18th cent.)

The Coolness

With one who can rule
   his words, and not speak all he thinks—
      I'm enjoying the cool!

HYAKUCHI (d. 1835)

Koi-shinaba | *waga* | *tsuka* | *de* | *nake* | *hototogisu*
Love-if-die-of | my | grave | at | cry | cuckoo

Koe | *bakari* | *ochite* | *ato* | *naki* | *hibari* | *kana*
Voice | only | falling | afterward | is-not | skylark | *kana*

Omou | *hodo* | *mono* | *iwanu* | *hito* | *to* | *suzumi-keri*
Think | extent-up-to | things | not-say | person | with | enjoy-cool-*keri*

Chapter VIII

ISSA

PERHAPS the best-loved of all the haiku poets is Issa (1762–1826). He was not a prophet like Bashō, nor a brilliant craftsman like Buson; he was just a very human man. But though Bashō himself was loved, his poetry is hard for most of us to understand without deep study; and Buson, brilliant as he was, had too detached a standpoint to induce affection. Issa, with all his frailties, wrote poetry that "opens his soul to us, therefore we love him."

Issa's life was on the whole a very sad one. His own mother died while he was still a baby, and his early days were embittered by a stepmother of the fairy-tale variety. The story goes that one day when Issa was about nine, there was a village festival for which all the other children got new clothes. Issa alone was in old and shabby things, and the other children would not play with him. While he was sitting apart, watching the fun, he saw a little fledgling sparrow,

which looked utterly forlorn, as if it had just fallen
from the nest. Turning to it, Issa said:

> Come! With each other
>   let's play—little sparrow
>   without any mother!

and burst into a storm of tears.

The original Japanese is too poignant, and too perfect, to have been composed by a child of nine, and
the probabilities are that Issa wrote it many years
later. It does, however, show the conditions of Issa's
childhood, and why his father thought it best for him
to leave home when he was about fourteen. For
twenty years Issa was away, with only one brief visit
home, mostly in Edo, sometimes gay and sometimes
sad, but always poor and unsuccessful. Then, just as
he was beginning to find success, his father died
(1801). Issa was with him at the time and was made
the principal heir, but his stepmother and half brother
would not recognize the will, and with the connivance
of the village authorities kept Issa out of his property
for nearly thirteen years. Issa returned to Edo, where
his talents gradually earned him the position he de-
served. But his heart yearned for his native place—he
was undoubtedly also influenced by desire for
property and dislike of his stepmother—and he returned several times to try and get matters straight-
ened out. It is not known on which of these journeys
he wrote:

Ore | *to* | *kite* | *asobe* | *yo* | *oya-no-nai* | *suzume*
Me | with | coming | play | ! | parent-less | sparrow

> The place where I was born:
> all I come to—all I touch—
> blossoms of the thorn.

but when one compares this poem to Buson's *Thorn* (page 109) one understands why Issa is loved and Buson is not. Issa is showing us the pain in his heart; Buson is speaking as a man of the world.

Issa finally got possession of his property and almost immediately left Edo and moved into it. At that time much of the bitterness seems to have left his heart, and as he himself says, he "became a new man." For his first New Year's Day at home (1814) he wrote:

> A strange, strange thing—
> in the house where I was born,
> this morning's spring!

In the same year he married Kiku, a village girl scarcely half his age, and lived with her in the house until her death ten years later. He seems to have been genuinely in love with her, but even this was not a very happy life, for he himself was often ill, and his five children by her all died young. It was in reference to one of them that he wrote:

Furusato | ya | yoru | mo | sawaru | mo | bara-no-hana
Old-village | : | come-near | also | touch | also |
thorn's-flowers

Furusato is the pure Japanese reading of the Sino-Japanese *kokyō* and is used of one's native place, whether or not it is really a village.

Fushigi | fushigi | umareta | ie | de | kesa-no | haru
Strange | strange | born-in | house | at | this-morning's |
spring

> A dewdrop fades away:
> "This world is dirty, and it has
>   no place for me."

It was on the death of another child that Issa wrote his most famous "dew" poem, one for which I can find no adequate English. As literally as possible it is:

> This Dewdrop World—
>   a dewdrop world it is, and still,
>   although it is . . .

The first line is taken from a scripture comparing the evanescence of life in the world with that of dew. But Issa is not thinking in generalities; he is suffering from the loss of his child. The feeling is much the same as in the previous poem, only much more powerfully expressed. A "Dew-World" though it is, it is no world for dewdrops. They will not stay in it—and, much as he tries to, he can find no solace in the scripture.

Issa's unhappiness seems to have been due to philosophical and religious unrest even more than to the actual hardships he endured. He did not have Buson's detachment and could not enter into Bashō's state of complete acceptance. He was not satisfied by the conventional Buddhism of the day; indeed he seems to have been a born rebel against all conventionality. His attitude toward life is probably best expressed by what has long been known as his "death poem":

Tsuyu | chiru | ya | musai | kono | yo | ni | yō | nashi | to
Dew | go away | : | dirty | this | world | in | business | is-none | [thus]

Tsuyu-no-yo | wa | tsuyu-no-yo | nagara | sari | nagara
Dew-world | as-for | dew-world | while-it-is | so-be | while-it-is

From washing bowl
to washing bowl my journey—
and just rigmarole!

Here the reference is to the basins used for a baby's first bath and at the washing of the body after death.

This poem was certainly not written on his deathbed but was probably given to one or more of his pupils to be published after his death. An attempt has even been made to question its authenticity, but the internal evidence seems far too strong. It has all of Issa's wry humor, and also the two levels of interpretation that mark nearly all of his best poems. On the surface it may be taken as meaning: "All my life I have done nothing but write stuff-and-nonsense"; on the deeper level that life may have meaning, but none that he can understand.

Issa's actual last poem was found under the pillow of the bed on which he died, deep in midwinter, in the windowless storage building he had moved into after his own house had burned down.

There are thanks to be given:
this snow on the bed quilt—
it too is from Heaven.

The Jōdo (Pure Land) he mentions is the heaven of the Buddha Amida, of whom it is told that while still a Bodhisattva (one ready to become a Buddha) he refused to enter Nirvana until the merit of his good works became so great that all men who should, in

Tarai | *kara* | *tarai* | *ni* | *utsuru* | *chimpunkan*
Basin | from | basin | to | shifting | jargon

Arigata | *ya* | *fusuma-no* | *yuki* | *mo* | *Jōdo* | *kara*
Thanks-due | : | bed-quilt's | snow | also | Pure-Land | from

faith, even call upon his name would find salvation
from the hells to which evil deeds condemned them.
Issa was a member of the largest of the Pure Land
sects, the Shin, and tried to be a devout one. The
boundless love attributed to Amida Buddha coalesced
with his own tenderness toward all weak things—
children and animals and insects. This was perhaps
the best part of him, and in all his poems about them
one feels that Issa identifies himself with his subject.
The famous and often translated haiku about the lean
frog:

> Lean frog,
>   don't give up the fight!
>   Issa is here!

is a typical example of such identification, as is also:

> Oh, don't mistreat
>   the fly! He wrings his hands!
>   He wrings his feet!

Issa, however, had no use for the conventional
Amidists, many of whom—mostly uneducated ones—
had twisted the original doctrine to mean that the
simple repetition of the formula "*Namu Amida Butsu*"
would save them from punishment for any sin, even
the great sin of taking life. And in one of his "fly"
haiku (he wrote many) Issa says:

Yase-gaeru | *makeru-na* | *Issa* | *koko-ni* | *ari*
Lean-frog | don't be-beaten | Issa | here | is

Yare-utsu-na | *hae* | *ga* | *te* | *wo* | *suru* | *ashi* | *wo* | *suru*
Don't-strike! | flies | [nom.] | hands | [acc.] | do | feet |
[acc.] | do

> For each single fly
>   that's swatted, "*Namu Amida
>   Butsu*" is the cry.

This of course is pure sarcasm but is redeemed by the amusing surface picture it calls up, of a pious family on a fly hunt.

Issa wrote many poems that show a strong feeling of natural religion, such as the following picture of the Hagi-Tamagawa at sunset:

> Bush-clover there,
>   now all in waves of color:
>   evening prayer!

But his formally religious ones give a curious effect of having been written primarily to convince himself that the only thing to do was to trust in Amida. Some of them are very moving, but I am not at all sure that I interpret him correctly, and so have not tried translation. The one that moves me most is very hard to put into English. It is the description of morning at a small country temple; there is at least some reason to believe that it was the one at which his children were buried:

Hae | hitotsu | uteba | Namu Amida Butsu | kana
Fly | one | when-strike | *Namu Amida Butsu* | kana

Hagi | mohaya | ironaru | nami | ya | yu | harai
Bush-clover | already | colored | waves | : | evening | prayer

There were six Tamagawa (Jewel Rivers) all celebrated in literature and art. This poem may be compared with the one by Bashō on p. 45.

Dew lies in teardrops,
and tenderly doves pray
to Buddha the Savior.

In the original the *horori horori* not only indicates tender compassion, a being moved to tears, but also gives the sound of the doves.

Issa's revolt against the social conventions of his time was bound to be fruitless and frustrating. He did not at all like the distinctions between high and low and rich and poor, but there was nothing effective he could do about them. We know that he used to go about in clothes much older and dirtier than even his poverty made necessary (at least until he was over fifty and his wife got after him), and that he used to be quite rude to great lords (*daimyō*) who tried to patronize him. But such behavior could hardly have brought him any real satisfaction. His feelings show through in many of his poems, as, for example:

A daimyō!—And who
makes *him* get off his horse?
Cherry blossoms do!

In the original the form makes the surface picture even more suggestive of praise to the cherries and recognition of the essential oneness of humanity. But when one remembers that the custom was that whenever a daimyō came along all other people had to get

Tsuyu | horori | horori | to | hata-no | nembutsu | kana
Dews | tearfully | tenderly | thus | pigeon's |
"Namu Amida Butsu" | kana

Daimyō | wo | uma | kara | orosu | sakura | kana
Daimyō | [acc.] | horse | from | make-get-down | cherries | kana

off their horses (if they had any) and squat by the side of the road—well, all the reader has to do is put himself in Issa's place.

Or take a very simple poem like his query to the children:

> What a red moon!
>   And whose is it,
>   children?

At first this seems to be simply an indirect way of saying that the great round moon looks like a child's toy—which it does. But when we go a little further, and take pleasure in the fact that it does not belong to anybody, we are ready to start a theory of economics if we want to.

Or such a poem as:

> They were called "Sir"
>   when they were being raised—
>   these silkworms were.

Silkworms were of vital economic importance to many Japanese households and, in recognition of the fact, were often given the title *sama,* a term of respect which can have more affectionate connotations than "sir." It would seem a kind of bringing-up to be envied, but Issa has used a verb form that indicates completion. The bringing-up is over; the worms are starting their cocoons, which most of them will never be allowed to leave alive.

Akai | *tsuki* | *kore* | *wa* | *taga-no* | *ja* | *kodomotachi*
Red | moon | this | as-for | whose | is-it | children

Sama-zuke | *ni* | *sodateraretaru* | *kaiko* | *kana*
"Sama"-stick-on | with | were-brought-up | silkworms | kana

Issa was also a rebel in the haiku world. His poems are—obviously—very different from any haiku that had been written before. In his own time he was actually driven out from his first position as a haiku teacher on account of his unconventionality, and even today there are those who claim that most of his work is not worthy of the name of haiku. Issa apparently felt the contemporary criticism keenly and spent a great deal of time polishing up a few poems that would meet the exacting standards of his critics. These few stick closely to the technical rules of the day but to me seem curiously thin when compared to the poems in which he really expresses his emotions. Probably the best one, the one of which Issa himself seems to have been proudest, is:

> There the spring passes—
> asway, aswing—look!—on the
> moorland, the grasses!

Speaking of Issa's own style as shown in his best poems (he did write quite a lot of poor ones), Mr. Ryusaku Tsunoda calls them two-dimensional, in contrast to Bashō's three-dimensional haiku, and the one-dimensional poems of Chiyo. I have previously spoken of two "levels," but in some ways "dimensions" is better, for Issa sometimes deliberately shifts the direction of an emotion into which the reader has been led. For instance, in one of his poems the first two lines are:

Yusa | yusa | to | haru-ga | yuku | zo ya | nobe-no-kusa
Sway | sway | thus | spring's | going | ! [Look!]! | moorland-grasses

> Snow melts,
>   and the village is overflowing—

This certainly starts one on a picture of disaster, which is suddenly—and delightfully—smashed by the last line:

> with children.

Issa uses much the same technique in one of his most often quoted poems—the one about the cherry festival at Ueno, where the cherry blossoms are still lovely, but in his time were still lovelier and used to be visited by milling thousands of picnickers. The first line has to be paraphrased. It means literally "blossoms' shadow," and arouses the image of a sunny day. But it also means, in common colloquial usage, "under their protection," "thanks to them."

> Thanks to cherry bloom,
>   in its shadow utter strangers—

In the original there is at this point a pause (*wa*), which gives us time to visualize the strangers, so that there is a pleasing unexpectedness about the ending:

> there are none!

It would be wrong, however, to give the reader the impression that Issa was a great technician or that all the verse he wrote was necessarily poetry. The use of tricks, especially using words with double meanings, can be carried too far, and such a "haiku" as this,

Yuki | *tokete* | *mura* | *ippai-no* | *kodomo* | *kana*
Snow | melting | village | "brimful" | children | *kana*

Hana-no | *kage* | *aka-no* | *tanin* | *wa* | *nakari-keri*
Blossoms' | shade | complete | strangers | as-for | do-not-exist-*keri*

apparently written after a visit home during the time he was trying to recover his property:

> The people? I can't say;
>   even an upright scarecrow
>   does not exist today.

is hardly poetry by any standards. But it does give us a nice picture of the fields full of scarecrows standing all awry, and a warm feeling for Issa as a man.

In most of his poems Issa tends to project himself and his own feelings into whatever he writes about, but his wording does not always show this. Issa probably realized the fact, as he had the habit of adding "—and Issa too" to his *haiga*. (*Haiga* are drawings accompanying a written haiku.) Thus for the poem:

> A garden butterfly;
>   the baby crawls, it flies . . .
>   she crawls, it flies. . . .

Issa has sketched a little thatched hut at the bottom, and at the end of the poem has added "The house, and Issa too." Here the device is necessary, for without it there is nothing to indicate that Issa is talking about his own child in his own garden and having the thoughts of a parent. But for such a poem as:

Hito | wa | iza | suguna | kagashi | mo | nakari-keri
People | as-for | not-say | upright | scarecrows | even | not-exist-*keri*

Suguna has the same double meaning as "upright."

Niwa-no-chō | ko | ga haeba | tobi | haeba | tobu
Garden-butterfly | child | [subj.] when-crawl | fly-and | when-crawl | fly

Once again in vain
   his mouth he opens—the bird's
      stepchild.

which is accompanied by a rough sketch of a rather
lopsided swallow, only those who know nothing of
Issa's background could need the added words: "The
swallow, and Issa too."

There are also other poems, for which even the
addition of "—and Issa too" is not enough. There is, for
example:

So hospitably
   waving at the entrance gate—
      the willow tree.

At first sight this is primarily a sympathetic description of a willow—which of course it is. But we can
appreciate Issa's feelings when he wrote the poem far
more deeply after we are told that there was a willow
at the entrance of his own house, from which he was
so long kept out by his stepmother.

Or take the poem written on the festival of the
Weaver Star (Vega) and her earth-born lover, the
Herdsman (Altair). It was celebrated throughout
Japan on the seventh day of the seventh month—ac-
cording to legend, the only day in the year on which
they are allowed to be together:

Mata | muda-ni | kuchi | wo | aku | tori-no | manako | kana
Again | uselessly | mouth | [acc.] | opens | bird's |
stepchild | *kana*

Iri-guchi-no | aiso | wo | nobiku | yanagi | kana
Entrance-gate's | hospitality | [acc.] | wave | willow |
kana

> Insects! Do not cry!
>   There are loves that have to part—
>   even in the sky.

It has an effect of lightness, perhaps even of over-sentimentality toward the insects. But from Issa's diary one learns that when it was written Issa's dearly loved wife, Kiku, was lying in her last illness, and once again Issa is tearing his heart out before us.

When Kiku did die Issa was utterly broken up. He wrote many poems about her, but the one that is most touching is completely incoherent as a haiku:

> A little child:
>   he starts to laugh, and—
>   autumn nightfall.

He knew himself that it was incoherent, and so prefaced it with a foreword saying "About a motherless child learning to crawl." As a slightly less incoherent paraphrase:

> The baby starts to crawl,
>   then stops, and laughs—the shades
>   of autumn fall.

Everything reminds him of his wife, but to hear her laughter from the mouth of her child is just too much to bear.

Naku-na | *mushi* | *wakaruru* | *koi* | *wa* | *hoshi* | *ni* | *sae*
Cry-not! | insects | get-parted | loves | as-for | stars | in | even

In the translation the rhyme "sky" is used instead of "stars," in order to keep the superficial effect of lightness found in the original.

Osanago | *ya* | *warau* | *ni* | *tsukete* | *aki-no-kure*
Little-child | : | laughter | by | taken | autumn-nightfall

Issa survived his wife about four years. Before he died he married again, apparently mainly for the purpose of having an heir. In this he succeeded, but with his typical combination of good luck and bad, for although the property he cared about so much is still in the hands of his descendants, his only surviving child, Yata, was born posthumously, so that he never saw her.

I hate to end this account of Issa on a note of sadness, and so am mentioning one more poem, which should be of particular interest to lovers of Japanese prints. It is written in very pompous and old-fashioned "epistolary" language (*sōrōbun*), which was then commonly used as speech only in stage performances.

> "He who appears
>   before you now—is the Toad
>   of this Thicket."

The point is that the position of a sitting toad is almost exactly like the one assumed by Japanese when they squat on the floor for formal greetings—the same one that actors would assume in introducing themselves to the audience at a formal *kaomise* ("face-showing").

Now, during Issa's time, there was in Edo a very famous theater manager, Miyako Dennai III, and one of the finest of Japanese prints is a portrait of him drawn by Toshūsai Sharaku in 1794.* He is shown

---

*It has been often reproduced. There is a very fine color reproduction in the catalogue of the Ledoux Collection (Part 4, No. 17, Princeton University Press, 1950. Two states, together with a fairly full discussion, are shown in *The Surviving Works of Sharaku*, Henderson and Ledoux (E. Weyhe, 1939).

Makari-idetaru | *wa* | *kono* | *yabu-no* | *gama* | *nite* | *sōrō*
Appearer-before-you | as-for | this | thicket's | toad | it-is

sitting, holding a paper with some lines in *sōrōbun;* he is a large, fat man, and looks very much like a toad. One cannot prove any connection, but one can at least take pleasure in the possibility.

New Year's Day

A new year starting, but—
   it's still just as it stands here,
      this ramshackle hut!

New-Year Presents

The New Year's gifts:
   even the baby at the breast
      puts out her little hands.

Late Snow

Seeming as though
   this must be the last of it—
      so much spring snow!

Gan-jitsu | mo | tachi-no-mamma-no | kuzu-ya | kana
Starting-day | even | just-as-it-stands | junk-house | *kana*

Toshi-dama | ya | futokoro-no-ko | mo | tete | wo | shite
"Year-jewels" | : | bosom-at-child | even | hand-waving | [acc.] | doing

Kore-kiri | to | miete | dossari | haru-no-yuki
This-the-end | thus | seeming | much | spring-snow

Spring Rain

Rain on a spring day:
  to the grove is blown a letter
    someone threw away.

The Long Spring Day

A day of spring—
  wherever any water is,
    in darkness lingering.

The Tempter

Plum blossoms swaying:
  "Here! Here! Steal this one!"—is that
    what the moon's saying?

Harusame | *ya* | *yabu* | *ni* | *fukaruru* | *sute-tegami*
Spring-rain | : | grove | to | get-blown | thrown-away-letter

A Japanese letter would be written on a single long
sheet of thin flexible paper.

Haru-no-hi | *ya* | *mizu* | *sae* | *areba* | *kure-nokori*
Spring-day | : | water | at-all | when-be |
dark-stay-through

The word *hi* is used also for "sun."

Ume-no-hana | *koko* | *wo* | *nusume* | *to* | *sasu* | *tsuki* | *ka*
Plum-blossoms | this-place | [acc.] | steal [!] | thus |
point | moon | ?

Nature Note

A bush warbler comes:
all muddy are the feet he wipes
upon the blooming plums.

An Old Folk Song

"Cherry blossoms! See!
Cherry bloom!"—and it was sung
of this old tree.

Cherry-Blossom Time

In my old home
which I forsook, the cherries
are in bloom.

Uguisu | ya | doro-ashi | nuguu | ume-no-hana
Warbler | : | **muddy-feet** | wipe | plum-blossoms

Sakura | sakura | to | utawareshi | oi-ki | kana
Cherry bloom | cherry bloom | thus | was-sung | old-tree | *kana*

Mikagirishi | furu-sato-no | sakura | saki-ni-keri
Ceased-to-see | old-village's | cherries | have-bloomed-*keri*

The Traveling Priest

A crossroad sermon! True,
  it's rigmarole—but then,
    it's tranquil too!

Spring

In the thicket's shade,
  and all alone, she's singing—
    the rice-planting maid.

The Mountain Stream

The mountain stream I use
  to pound the rice for me, while I
    take a noonday snooze.

Tsuji | *dangi* | *chimpunkan* | *mo* | *nodoka* | *kana*
Crossroads | sermon | rigmarole | even[being] |
tranquillity | *kana*

Yabu-kage | *ya* | *tatta* | *hitori-no* | *ta-ue-uta*
Thicket-shadow | : | just | alone's | rice-planting-song

Yama-mizu | *ni* | *kome* | *wo* | *tsukasete* | *hiru-ne* | *kana*
Mountain-water | to | rice | [acc.] | causing-to-strike |
noon-nap | *kana*

Conscience

Somehow it seems wrong:
    to take one's noonday nap and hear
      a rice-planting song.

A Warning

Little sparrow! Take care!
    Get out of the way!—Mr. Horse
      is coming there!

The Great Buddha at Nara

Out from the hollow
    of Great Buddha's nose—
      comes a swallow.

Motaina | *ya* | *hiru-ne* | *shite* | *kiku* | *ta-ue-uta*
Impiety | : | noon-nap | doing | hear | rice-planting-song

Suzume-no | *ko* | *soko-noke* | *soko-noke* | *o-ume-ga* | *tōru*
Sparrow's | child | out-of-the-way! | out-of-the-way |
Mr. Horse's | coming-through

Dai-butsu-no | *hana* | *kara* | *izuru* | *tsubame* | *kana*
Great Buddha's | nose | from | come-out | swallow | *kana*

A bronze figure fifty-two feet high, cast in the eighth
century but much repaired, and now the ugliest statue in
Japan, with great flaring nostrils.

In the Field

Tilling the field?—Just so
    does he act as he walks there,
        the crow!

In the House

At the butterflies
    the caged bird gazes, envying—
        just watch its eyes!

The Cat

Sleeping, then waking
    and giving a great yawn, the cat
        goes out love-making.

Hata-uchi-no | *mane* | *wo* | *shite* | *aruku* | *karasu* | *kana*
Dry-field-tilling's | imitation | [acc.] | doing | walk | crow | *kana*

Kago-no-tori | *chō* | *wo* | *urayamu* | *me-tsuki* | *kana*
Caged-bird | butterflies | [acc.] | envy | eye-expression | *kana*

Nete | *okite* | *ō-akubi* | *shite* | *neko-no* | *koi*
Sleeping | getting-up | great-yawn | doing | cat's | loving

A Summer Day

High noon:
    save for reed-sparrows, the river
      makes no sound.

The Road Home

On the Shinano road,
    such heat! The very mountains
      turn into a load!

Summer Rain

A sudden shower falls—
    and naked I am riding
      on a naked horse!

Hizakari | *ya* | *yoshi* | *kiri-ni* | *kawa-no* | *oto* | *mo* | *nashi*
High-noon | : | reed-sparrows | save-for | river's | sound | even | is-not

Shinano-ji-no | *yama-ga* | *ni-ni-naru* | *atsusa* | *kana*
Shinano-road's | mountain's | burden-turn-into | heat | kana

   Shinano was Issa's home province. His journeys home
were usually unhappy ones.

Yū-dachi | *ya* | *hadaka-de* | *norishi* | *hadake-uma*
Sudden-shower | : | being-naked | had-got-on | naked-horse

Contentment in Poverty

A one-foot waterfall—
   it too makes noises,
      and at night is cool.

Issa's Guests

If the times were good,
   I'd say: "One more of you, sit down,
      flies around my food!"

Waiting

A man, just one—
   also a fly, just one—
      in the huge drawing room.

Is-shaku-no | *taki* | *mo* | *oto* | *shite* | *yū-suzumi*
One-foot | waterfall | also | sound | making | evening-cool

Yo | *ga* | *yokuba* | *mo-hitotsu* | *tomare* | *meshi-no* | *hae*
World | [subj.] | if-be-good | one-more | settle-down |
meal's | flies

Hito | *hitori* | *hae* | *hitotsu* | *ya* | *ō-zashiki*
Person | one | fly | one | : | large-guest-room

Summer Heat

The locust-shrill:
  precisely a red paper
    toy windmill!

The Firefly

A giant firefly:
  that way, this way, that way, this—
    and it passes by.

The Line of Ants

The roadway of the ants:
  it starts from the far cloud-peaks
    and stretches here, perchance.

Semi | *naku* | *ya* | *tsuku-zuku* | *akai* | *kaze-guruma*
Locusts | cry | : | exactly | red | wind-wheel

Ō-hotaru | *yurari-yurari* | *to* | *tōri-keri*
Big-firefly | waver-waver | thus | pass-through-*keri*

Ari-no | *michi* | *kumo-no-mine* | *yori* | *tsuzukiken*
Ant's | road | cloud-peaks | from | may-continue
  "Cloud-peaks" are white cumulus clouds on the horizon.

The Deep Gorge

On hands and knees I go
   across the rope bridge, and a cuckoo
   starts singing—from below!

A Meeting

Right at my feet—
   and when did you get here,
   snail?

The Snail

Snail, my little man,
   slowly, oh, very slowly
   climb up Fujisan!

Hai-wataru | *hashi-no* | *shita* | *yori* | *hototogisu*
Crawling-cross | bridge's | underneath | from | cuckoo

Ashimoto | *e* | *itsu* | *kitarishi* | *yo* | *katatsumuri*
Foot-base | to | when | did-arrive | ? ! | snail

Katatsuburi | *soro* | *soro* | *nobore* | *Fuji-no-yama*
Snail | slowly | slowly | climb-up | Fuji-mountain

The famous peak is known either as *Fuji-no-yama* (Fuji-mountain or Fuji-san Mt. Fuji). The western name "Fuji-yama" is unknown in Japan.

The Unlocked Gate

A brushwood gate:
in place of a lock—
this snail.

The Vision

In its eye
are mirrored far-off mountains—
dragonfly!

Moor Hens

The moor hens sing,
and to their tempo—look!—the clouds
are hurrying.

Shiba-no-to | *ya* | *jō-no-kawari-ni* | *katatsumuri*
Brushwood-gate | : | lock-in-place-of | snail

Tō-yama-no | *me-dama* | *ni* | *utsuru* | *tombo* | *kana*
Distant-mountains' | eye-jewels | in | reflect | dragonfly |
kana

Kuina | *naku* | *hyoshi* | *ni* | *kumo-ga* | *isogu* | *zo yo*
Moor hens | sing | tempo | to | clouds' | hurrying |
! [look] !

Repairs

A morning-glory vine,
all blossoming, has thatched
this hut of mine.

Retirement

My hermitage:
the frogs here, from the very start
have chanted of old age.

Long Autumn Night

Fleas! Surely you too
must find the night long!
You too seem lonely!

Asagao-no | hana | de | fuitaru | ioi | kana
Morning-glories' | flowers | with | has-been-thatched |
hut | *kana*

Waga | io | ya | kawazu | shote-kara | oi | wo | naku
My | retreat | : | frogs | beginning-from | old-age | [acc.] |
sing

Nomi-domo | mo | yo-naga | darō | zo | sabishikaro
Fleas | also | "night's-length | it-probably-is | ! |
lonely-seem

The Passing of Youth

Old, and crippled by years
    do I seem?—Even mosquitoes
        buzz close to my ears!

The New Moon

Just three days old,
    the moon, and it's all warped and bent!
        How keen the cold!

The Mushroom

Death it can bring,
    that kind of mushroom; and, of course,
        it's a pretty thing.

Toshi-yori | *to* | *mite-ya* | *naku* | *ka* | *mo* | *mimi-no-soba*
Aged-person | thus | do-they-see-me? | buzzing | gnats |
even | ears-close-to

Mikazuki | *wa* | *soru* | *zo* | *samusa* | *wa* | *saekaeru*
Three-day-moon | as-for | be-curved | ! | cold | as-for |
is-very-strong

Hito | *wo* | *toru* | *kinoko* | *hatashite* | *utsukushii*
People | [acc.] | kill | mushroom | of-course | is-pretty

The Passing of Autumn

Autumn goes away,
    and the tail-flower's waving plumes—
        "Good-by!" "Good-by!" they say.

Pampas Grass

Withered pampas grass:
    "Well, once upon a time,
        an old witch there was . . ."

A Temple

The mountain temple here:
    from its covered porches come
        voices of deer. . . .

Yuku | aki | wo | obana | ga | saraba | saraba | kana
Going | autumn | [to] | "tailflower" | [subj.] | good-by |
good-by | kana

The *obana*, here literally translated as "tail-flower," is
another name for the *susuki*, a wild eulalia with plumes
much like those of pampas grass.

Kare-susuki | mukashi | oni-baba | atta | to | sa
Withered-pampas-grass | once-upon-a-time | old-witch |
there-was | thus | it-is

Yama-dera | ya | en-no-ue-naru | shika-no | koe
Mountain-temple | : | veranda-on-being | deers' | voices

Heaven's River

A lovely thing to see:
through the paper window's hole,
the Galaxy.

A Wish

My grumbling wife—
if only she were here!
This moon tonight . . .

Winter

Now that I'm old
I am envied by people—
Oh, but it's cold!

Utsukushi | *ya* | *shōji-no* | *ana-no* | *Ama-no-gawa*
Lovely | : | sliding-door's | hole's | Heavenly-River

Ko-goto | *iu* | *aite* | *mo* | *araba* | *kyō-no-tsuki*
"Small-words" | saying | companion | also | if-be-here |
today's-moon

Toshikasa | *wo* | *urayametaru* | *samusa* | *kana*
Old-age | [acc.] | being-envied | cold | *kana*

Chapter IX

SHIKI

THE greater part of the nineteenth century was a bad time for haiku. When Issa died he left no real school behind him, and Buson's followers, lacking his dynamic personality, fell more and more into an artificiality comparable to that which had existed before the advent of Bashō. The revolt against this artificiality took place in the closing years of the century, under the banner of Masaoka Shiki (1867–1902).

Japan was at that time still in the throes of change, with the old order everywhere in conflict with new ideas imported from the West; and Shiki was peculiarly fitted, by both training and temperament, to be a leader in the literary revolution. The Meiji restoration had taken place in 1868, and during Shiki's boyhood days Japan was full of alarms and excursions, culminating in the Satsuma Rebellion of 1877. Before this time Shiki had already started school—had started several schools, in fact, for his education seems to have been peculiarly scrappy—and there can be little doubt that the circumstances of his early life did much to confirm him in the restlessness that was one of his later characteristics.

Shiki was exceedingly precocious. He began writing when he was about eleven, the year before he graduated to the middle school, and continued to write, in family poetry contests and the like, until he was sixteen, when he left his country school and went to Tokyo. Here he started the study of haiku seriously, and it was not long before he first tried his hand at professional writing. At this time he was not in good health and was not receiving any formal education, though he did attend lectures at the university. When he was twenty-one he showed signs of tuberculosis, and was too ill even to graduate from middle school until two years later. He then entered college, but failed in his second-year examinations and shortly after went on the staff of the newspaper *Nihon*, to which he had done some previous contributing. Here his writings attracted considerable attention, and he had been with the paper less than a year when he startled the haiku world by his famous "Criticism of Bashō."

This criticism makes very curious reading. It is not really an attack on Bashō so much as an expression of youthful intolerance with honoring old things just because they are old. Nevertheless, though Shiki admits that some of Bashō's poems are really very great, he does state definitely that at least four fifths of them are bad—and to most of his readers this must have sounded like pure blasphemy. Probably this is just what Shiki intended, and it certainly did have the effect of getting his articles discussed. It is only fair to say that later in life he considerably revised his early opinions.

Other articles followed in quick succession, and Shiki soon had a band of active supporters—most of them eager young poets like himself—to help him in his crusade. The beginnings were naturally attacks on the established order, especially on the stultifying over-veneration for rules of composition supposed to have been laid down by great masters of the past; and joined with this was a somewhat chaotic desire for something new. Two hundred years before, Ransetsu had written a famous haiku:

> Yellow chrysanthemums!
>> White chrysanthemums! Other names—
>> would that there were none!

Shiki's reply to this:

> Chrysanthemums! True,
>> yellow ones, white ones—but I want
>> a red one too!

can be taken as exemplifying their point of view. Shiki, however, was not long satisfied with tearing down. He wished to build up as well and to lay the foundations for a new school of haiku. In this he succeeded, and his advice, most of it given first in his newspaper articles, had a very great and salutary influence.

The chief points in his advice to beginners are:

Ki-giku | shira-giku | sono | hoka-no | na | wa | naku-mogana

Yellow chrysanthemums | white chrysanthemums | besides | name | as-for | would-there-were-not

Kigiku | shira-giku | hito | moto | wa | aka | mo | aramahoshi

Yellow chrysanthemums | white chrysanthemums | one | "base" | as-for | red | also | I-want

Be natural.

Don't bother about old rules of grammar and special points like spelling, *kireji*, etc.

Read the old authors, remembering that in them you will find good and bad poems mixed.

Notice that commonplace haiku are not direct, but artificially twisted out of shape.

Write to please yourself. If your writings do not please yourself, how can you expect them to please anybody else?

It will be noticed that all this advice is simply "Be natural" repeated in a number of different ways.

To those who know something about haiku but are not yet masters—and of these there are still many hundreds of thousands in Japan—Shiki had much to say. The following is an outline:

Remember perspective. Large things are large, but small things are also large if seen close up.

Delicacy should be studied, but it cannot be applied to human affairs in seventeen syllables. It can be applied to natural objects.

Haiku are not logical propositions, and no process of reasoning should show on the surface.

Keep the words tight; put in nothing useless.

Cut down as much as possible on adverbs, verbs, and "postpositions."

Use both imaginary pictures and real ones, but prefer the real ones. If you use imaginary pictures you will get both good and bad haiku, but the good ones will be very rare. If you use real pictures, it is

still difficult to get very good haiku, but it is comparatively easy to get second-class ones, which will
keep some value even after the lapse of years.

Shiki's advice to the third class, those who are
already haiku masters, is perhaps even more interesting for what it does not say than for what it does. The
gist of it is:

Read, whenever you can, all worth-while books
on haiku; think over their good and their bad points.

Know all kinds of haiku, but have your own style.

Gather new material directly; do not take it from
old haiku.

Know something about other literature also.

Know at least something about all art.

The practical results of this advice have been excellent, but that it should have been thought necessary,
and even revolutionary, certainly shows the depths to
which haiku had fallen.

In 1895, after Shiki had returned from China, where
he had had a short term as a war correspondent, his
new school of haiku was formally recognized and became known as the "Nihon School." Two years later
he and his associates founded the monthly magazine
Hototogisu (*The Cuckoo*), which became the most in-
fluential haiku publication in Japan. The name seems
to have been suggested by one of Shiki's own haiku:

> To ears
>   defiled by sermons—
>   a cuckoo.

Sekkyo | *ni* | *kegareta* | *mimi* | *wo* | *hototogisu*
Sermon | by | dirtied | ears | [acc.] | cuckoo

Although Shiki was an avowed agnostic, this haiku is not so much an attack on religion as it is on hypocrisy and addiction to meaningless forms, and so, by extension, an attack on the classicists.

In the same year Shiki wrote an article on Buson, comparing him to Bashō and claiming that while many of Bashō's haiku were poor, all of Buson's were good. The reason for this extravagant praise seems to have been that Buson, in spite of much obvious artificiality, was a conscious innovator and a master stylist, and that therefore Shiki considered him at least in these respects a good model for his own new school. Certainly Shiki himself was much influenced by Buson's technique, and several of his poems were obviously inspired by the work of the earlier master. They are not copies, and the differences are often very revealing. For example, Buson had written:

> On the temple bell
>   has settled, and is fast asleep,
>   a butterfly.

and Shiki has a poem:

> On the temple bell
>   has settled, and is glittering,
>   a firefly.

The technique is exactly the same; the feeling conveyed is completely different.

Shiki's lack of appreciation of Bashō seems to have been due to a basic difference of temperament. Shiki

Tsurigane | ni | tomarite | nemuru | kochō | kana
Temple-bell | on | settling | sleeps | butterfly | *kana*

Tsurigane | ni | tomarite | hikaru | hotaru | kana
Temple-bell | on | settling | glitters | firefly | *kana*

had a restlessness to which Bashō's serenity could not appeal. And this was aggravated by Shiki's youth; he was still in his twenties when he wrote his two famous attacks on Bashō, and nearly all of Bashō's finest haiku were written after the age of forty. It has been claimed that it was Shiki's agnosticism that made him dislike Bashō; but this is questionable. Other agnostics have admired Bashō, and Shiki seems to have been as little satisfied with his own agnosticism as he was with Buddhism, or Shintoism, or such Christianity as he had come across. Several of his poems show that he felt lack of faith to be a cold, sad thing; the clearest of these is perhaps:

> The autumn wind:
> > for me there are no gods;
> > there are no Buddhas.

After the foundation of *Hototogisu,* Shiki was a very busy man. He was the leader of a new movement, which he felt had to be firmly established. He was not only writing his own poetry, but also many newspaper and magazine articles, and in addition to his normal editorial duties he took on the job of literary editor, which meant that he personally had to go through all the thousands of haiku that were being submitted for publication every month. He took his duties seriously and it is no wonder that his health, never very strong, broke down under the strain. Incidentally, his health was also affected by an inordinate liking for persimmons—the older Japanese variety, rather astringent— of which he ate far too many, so that he had to be restricted to a specified number per day. One has to

Aki-kaze | *ya* | *ware-ni* | *kami* | *nashi* | *hotoke* | *nashi*
Autumn-wind | : | to-me | gods | are-not | Buddhas | are-not

know this to appreciate the humor of one of his poems of the period:

> Haiku! Reading through
> three thousand, I have here
> persimmons—two!

The last few years of Shiki's life were very sad ones. He was in constant pain from his tuberculosis and an affliction of the spine, and for much of the time was confined to his sickbed. Until he died he continued to take an interest in writing, and during his illness he helped to start a number of magazines on poetry. But in most of his writings of this period one feels the cry of "I am in pain!" repeated and repeated until the constant iteration produces an agony almost too great for even the reader to bear.

> At still-living eyes
> have they come here to prick?
> These ever-restless flies!

and:

> The next room's light,
> that too goes out, and now—
> the chill of night.

Shiki died in 1902 at the age of thirty-five.

Sanzen-no | haiku | wo | etsushi | kaki | futatsu
Three-thousand | haiku | [acc.] | inspecting | persimmons | two

Ikita | me | wo | tsutsuki-ni | kuru | ka | hae-no | tobu
Alive | eyes | [acc.] | to-pick-at | come | ? | flies' | flying

Tsugi-no | ma-no | tomoshi | mo | kiete | yo-samu | kana
Next | room's | light | also | going-out | night-cold | *kana*

During his life Shiki was a dedicated man. As a poet he wanted as many people as possible to write as many haiku as possible. But they must be good haiku, and that meant that not only must the technique be good; above all, they must be records of genuine emotion. The drive behind this, however, was his love for Japan. Shiki, as a patriot should, wanted to preserve all that was best in the old national culture, and he found himself opposed by a strong "foreign" party —undoubtedly patriots too, but much misguided—who wished to take over Western culture in its entirety.

Shiki loved his country—its scenery, its people, its customs, its history, its traditions—and he wrote about them constantly and much more consciously than previous haiku masters. His poems about Japan are likely to be among his finest, because in these his emotion is not only genuine, but also strong. They do, however, present special difficulties to foreigners. Sometimes these difficulties can be cleared up by explanation. Take for example:

> Of those who pass
> with spears erect, there are none.
> Plumes of pampas grass.

Here the reference is to the daimyō processions that in the days of the Tokugawa Shogunate used to go regularly between Edo and the provinces. Shiki himself had never seen them, but many older Japanese had, and must have often described them to him. They can be visualized from illustrations, such as those by Hiroshige, who had died less than twenty years before Shiki's birth. These show a long cortege of retainers,

Yari | tatete | tōru | hito | nashi | hana-susuki
Spears | holding-up | go-through | persons | are-not | flowering-pampas-grass

not all spearmen, and among them a number carrying
long poles with colored tufts at the end, which acted
as identifying standards. It was probably such standards, rather than the spears themselves, which the
pampas plumes suggested to Shiki's mind.

Or take as another example:

> Atsumori's tomb—
>   and here there is not even
>   a cherry tree to bloom!

Every literate Japanese would know of Atsumori, a
gallant young samurai of the twelfth century who was
killed in battle at the age of fifteen, and would in-
stantly recognize the traditional connection between
such young samurai and falling cherry blossoms—a
connection so strong that Shiki did not even have to
mention the blossoms. And most of all, he would feel,
with Shiki, the wickedness of letting the past go
wholly into oblivion.

There are, however, many haiku for which no
amount of explanation will suffice. It is possible to get
some sort of an emotion from a haiku like:

> To rain-clouds
>   it calls, "Onward!"—the banner
>   in the storm.

But the "banner" is not a European one; it is very long
and narrow and is fastened to the top of a high pole;
without having seen it one cannot visualize its signal
to the rain clouds. And even the movement indicated

Atsumori-*no* | *haka* | *ni* | *sakura* | *mo* | *nakarikeri*
Atsumori's | tomb | at | cherry [tree] | even | there-is-not

Ama-gumo | *wo* | *sasou* | *arashi-no* | *nobori* | *kana*
Rain-clouds | [acc.] | inviting | storm's | banner | *kana*

by the verb is a peculiarly Japanese one. (Incidentally, *sasou*, which is here translated as "draw onward" has a basic meaning of "urge to go along with one.")

And, what can one do with this, which is deservedly one of Shiki's most famous poems:

> Persimmons: as I chew,
> a temple bell begins to boom
> from Hōryū.

It is possible to explain that Hōryū Temple (Hōryū-ji) dates from the seventh century; that it is the oldest wooden building in the world; that it contains wonderful old wall paintings and sculptures; that it has been venerated for ages. It is possible to explain that Shiki liked persimmons; that Shiki's persimmons did not have the same taste or consistency as Western ones; that their slight astringency is indicated by the "k" sounds in the first line *kaki kueba;* etc., etc. But no foreigner can have quite the same feeling about Hōryū-ji that a Japanese has; and how can anyone get the subtle connection—and there is one—between a taste he has never tasted and a sound he has never heard?

Of course, Shiki did not always write poems that are purely nationalistic. Such a poem as:

> Treading the clouds,
> inhaling the mist:
> a soaring skylark.

Kaki | kueba | kane | ga | naru | nari | Hōryū-ji
Persimmons | when-eat | bell | 's | peal | it-is | Hōryū-Temple

Kumo | wo | fumi | kasumi | wo | suu | ya | age-hibari
Clouds | [acc.] | treading | mist | [acc.] | inhaling | : | soaring-skylark

might have been written by any real poet, no matter what his nationality. So perhaps might the following description of a spring concert:

> On how to sing
>   the frog school and the skylark school
>   are arguing.

though it does gain added point from the fact that its author had founded what was sometimes called the "Cuckoo School."

Shiki was very fond of using the purely objective type of haiku, the effect of which he likened to that of a painting.

> One full moon;
>   stars numberless; the sky
>   dark green.

If anyone should ask what this "means," Shiki has already answered that only a tyro asks what a poem "means"; the only thing that matters is what effect it has. And certainly in such a poem as this, where Shiki is writing about universals, both foreigners and Japanese can get the same picture and the same effect.

Even when outsiders do not get quite the same picture that a Japanese would, it usually does not matter too much.

Hibari-ha | *to* | *kaeru-ha* | *to* | *uta-no* | *giron* | *kana*
Skylark-school | [and] | frog-school | [and] | song's | discussion | *kana*

Tsuki | *ichi-rin* | *hoshi* | *mu-kazu* | *sora* | *midori* | *kana*
Moon | one-circle | stars | un-numbered | sky | [dark] green | *kana*

Far peaks of cloud—
   white sails that in the south
      together crowd.

Once we know that "cloud-peaks" refer, by convention, to white cumulus clouds on the horizon, we can get the picture. It is summer, and from some high point we are looking out across the open sea; it does not matter what shape the sails are, or even whether they are real. (It so happens that to me the setting is England, centuries ago, and I get a sense of youthful dreams of Raleigh and of Drake. Shiki of course could not possibly have meant this, but I am sure he would not mind.)

The real trouble comes when Shiki gives the description of a purely Japanese scene—which he usually does. No foreigner, unless he has lived most of his life in Japan, can visualize it clearly; and unless one can get the picture, it is impossible to get the underlying emotion.

Through the center of the town
   flows a little river; here
      willow trees hang down.

For this even the translation has to have redundant words like "hang down" to show that the trees are weeping willows. The town is certainly very different from any town in Europe or America. As I visualize it,

Kumo-no-mine | *shira-ho* | *minami* | *ni* | *muragareri*
Cloud-peaks | white-sails | south | in | crowding-together

Machi-naka | *wo* | *o-gawa* | *nagaruru* | *yanagi* | *kana*
Town-center | [acc.] | little-stream | flowing | willows | *kana*

in Shiki's time "modern improvements" are creeping
in. There is probably a factory; almost surely electric-
light or telegraph poles; and only the river and the
willows to keep the original closeness to nature. But I
may be wrong.

It is a great pity that we non-Japanese cannot appreciate more of these poems, because the technique of
purely objective word painting is a very good one,
and Shiki used it to perfection. By means of it he
could run the gamut of emotion, from the most delicate suggestiveness to powerful, stark realism. On the
one hand we have a poem like:

> Evening moon:
>   plum blossoms start to fall
>   upon the lute.

The *koto* (here called "lute") is really a Chinese in-
strument, usually played by ladies, so that the scene
might be in China as well as Japan. But no player is
mentioned—she is not there—and the original gives a
curious feeling of romantic and almost unreal expectancy.

And at the other end of the scale Shiki can give us
pictures like:

> In the winter river,
>   thrown away, a dog's
>   dead body.

Yū-zuki | *ya* | *ume* | *chiri-kakaru* | *koto-no-ue*
Evening-moon | : | plums | start-to-fall | *koto's*-top

Fuyu-gawa | *ni* | *sutetaru* | *inu-no* | *kabane* | *kana*
Winter-river | in | thrown-away | dog's | carcass | *kana*

One does not have to be a Japanese to feel in this a cold deeper than that of any winter.

Shiki died before his powers reached their full maturity, but before he died he and his colleagues had won the battle against artificiality and had brought to haiku a new sense of youth and freshness. It is possible that the victory went too far. Shiki had a habit of using haiku to record any genuine emotion, no matter how ephemeral or unimportant it might be, and to me it seems that this habit resulted in his publishing a great deal of very second-rate verse. But this, of course, is the judgment of a foreigner.

I have emphasized the special difficulties that Shiki presents, partly because I feel that my own translations do an even greater injustice to him than to the other haiku masters. Much of the pleasure one gets from his poetry depends on its style, which is clear-cut like an intaglio and practically impossible to retain in translation. To the following examples of his work I have added a dozen haiku by his contemporaries and followers. These are not properly representative of their work—which really deserves a book of its own—but are simply those which in desultory reading I happen to have come across and to have liked.

A Spring Day

A day of spring:
    a hamlet where not anyone
      is doing anything.

Haru-no-hi | *ya* | *hito* | *nanimo* | *senu* | *ko-mura* | *kana*
Spring-day | : | person | anything | not-do | small-village | kana

Spring Road

Backward I gaze;
   one whom I had chanced to meet
     is lost in haze.

On Reading the Manyōshu

And no one knows
   who wrote it—this springtime
     master-song.

"Buddha's Tower Stands on Nothingness"

The mists come;
   the mountains fade and vanish;
     the tower stands alone.

Kaeri-mireba | yuki-aishi | hito | kasumi-keri
When-look-back | had-run-across | person |
become-hazy-*keri*

Yomibito | wo | shirazaru | haru-no | shū-ka | kana
Author | [acc.] | not-be-known | spring's | master-song |
kana

  The *Man-yō-shu* (*Collection of Ten Thousand Leaves*)
is Japan's oldest book of poems and was compiled in the
eighth century.

Kasumi-keri | yama | kie-usete | tō | hitotsu
Become-hazy-*keri* | mountains | fade-vanishing | tower |
one

Treasure-Trove

A long-forgotten thing:
a pot where now a flower blooms—
this day of spring!

The Moor

Spring moor:
for what do people go, for what
do they return?

Cherry-Viewing at Ueno

Coming to see cherry bloom
he had his money stolen—
the country bumpkin.

Wasure-ori-shi | hachi | ni | hana | saku | haru-hi | kana
Had-been-forgotten | pot | in | flower | bloom |
spring-day | *kana*

Haru-no-no | ya | nani-ni | hito | yuku | hito | kaeru
Spring-moor | : | what-for | people | go | people | return

Hana | ni | kite | zeni | torarare-keri | inaka-bito
Blossoms | to | coming | money | got-stolen |
country-person

At Matsushima

Islands all around,
    each with its pine trees; and the wind—
        how cool its sound!

Coolness

The plan to steal
    melons, that's forgotten too—
        how cool I feel!

After the Storm

The thunderstorm goes by;
    on one tree evening sunlight—
        a cicada cry.

Shima | *areba* | *matsu* | *ari* | *kaze-no* | *oto* | *suzushi*
Islands | when-are | pines | are | wind's | sound | is-cool

Uri | *nusumu* | *koto* | *mo* | *wasurete* | *suzumi* | *kana*
Melons | steal | affair | too | forgetting | coolness | *kana*

Rai | *harete* | *ichi-jū-no* | *yū-hi* | *semi-no* | *koe*
Thunder | clearing-up | one-tree's | evening-sun | locust's |
voice

Summer Evening

The moon begins to rise
  behind the grasses; a wind stirs them;
    and a cuckoo cries.

Summer Night

A lightning flash:
  between the forest trees
    I have seen water.

The Prayer

A prayer for rain:
  "To heaven be it echoed!"—thus go
    the beating drums.

Tsuki-no | *de-no* | *kusa* | *ni* | *kaze* | *fuku* | *hototogisu*
Moon's | out-coming's | grasses | in | wind | blow | cuckoo

Inazuma | *ya* | *mori-no* | *sukima* | *ni* | *mizu* | *wo* | *mitari*
Lightning | : | forest's | opening | in | water | [acc.] |
have-seen

Ama-goi | *ya* | *ten* | *ni* | *hibike* | *to* | *utsu* | *taiko*
Rain-prayer | : | heaven | to | resound | thus | beating |
drums

Heat

The summer river:
  although there is a bridge, my horse
    goes through the water.

The Old Priest

A temple in the hills:
  the snoring from a noon siesta—
    and a cuckoo's trills.

A Graveyard

A graveyard: low
  the grave mounds lie, and rank
    the grasses grow.

Natsu-kawa | *ya* | *hashi* | *are-do* | *uma* | *mizu* | *wo* | *yuku*
Summer-river | : | bridge | though-there-is | horse | water |
[acc.] | goes

Yama-dera | *ya* | *hiru-ne-no* | *ibiki* | *hototogisu*
Mountain-temple | : | noon-sleep's | snoring | cuckoo

Haka-bara | *ya* | *haka* | *hikuku-shite* | *kusa* | *shigeru*
Grave-yard | : | graves | being-low | grasses | are-rank

Waiting

Night; and once again,
    the while I wait for you, cold wind
        turns into rain.

After the Fireworks

The others go home.
    With the fireworks over,
        how dark it's become!

A Shinto Shrine

A shrine: here, keeping
    far from the garden lights,
        float wild birds, sleeping.

Kimi | *matsu* | *yo* | *mata* | *kogarashi-no* | *ame* | *ni* | *naru*
You | await | night | again | cold-wind's | rain | to |
becoming

Hito | *kaeru* | *hanabi-no* | *ato-no* | *kuraki* | *kana*
People | go-home | fireworks' | afterward | be-dark | *kana*

Miyashiro | *ya* | *niwa-hi* | *ni* | *toki* | *uki-ne-dori*
Shrine | : | garden-lights | to | be-far | float-sleep-birds

At Kamakura

The Great Buddha! Not at all
  does he blink an eyelid—
    as the hailstones fall.

In the Moonlight

It looks like a man,
  the scarecrow in the moonlit night—
    and it is pitiful.

The New and the Old

Railroad tracks; a flight
  of wild geese close above them
    in the moonlit night.

Dai-butsu-no | *majiroki* | *mo* | *se-nu* | *arare* | *kana*
Great-Buddha's | blinking | even | not-doing | hailstones |
kana

Hito | *ni* | *nite* | *tsuki-yo-no* | *kagashi* | *aware* | *nari*
Human | to | being-like | moon-night's | scarecrow |
pitiful | is

Ki-sha-michi | *ni* | *hikuku* | *kari* | *tobu* | *tsuki-yo* | *kana*
Steam-car-road | at | low | geese | fly | moon-night | *kana*

Medieval Scene

Eleven of them go,
  horsemen who do not turn their heads—
    through the wind-blown snow.

Winter

A mountain village:
  under the piled-up snow
    the sound of water.

The Apprentice Priestling

A boy not ten years old
  they are giving to the temple!
    Oh, it's cold!

Jūik-ki | *omote* | *mo* | *furanu* | *fu-buki* | *kana*
Eleven-riders | faces | even | not-swing | blown-snow |
kana

Yama-zato | *ya* | *yuki* | *tsumu-no* | *shita-no* | *mizu-no-oto*
Mountain-village | : | snow | pile-up's | under's |
water-sound

To | *ni* | *taranu* | *ko* | *wo* | *tera* | *ni* | *yaru* | *samusa* | *kana*
Ten | to | not-reach | child | [acc.] | temple | to | give |
coldness | *kana*

A Solitary Grave

Icy the moonshine:
  shadow of a tombstone,
    shadow of a pine.

After Rain

Clearing after showers,
  and for a little while the scent
    of hawthorn flowers . . .

KYOSHI

The Snake

A snake! Though it passes,
  eyes that had glared at me
    stay in the grasses.

KYOSHI

Kan-getsu | *ya* | *seki-tō-no* | *kage* | *matsu-no* | *kage*
Cold-moon | : | grave-stone's | shadow | pine's | shadow

Ame | *harete* | *shibaraku* | *bara-no* | *nioi* | *kana*
Rain | clearing-up | for-a-while | thorn's | scent | *kana*

Hebi | *nigete* | *ware* | *wo* | *mishi* | *me-no* | *kusa-ni* | *nokoru*
Snake | fleeing | me | [acc.] | had-looked-at | eyes' | grass-in | remain

In the Darkness

Because they pain
  my eyes, no lamps are lit tonight.
    The Maytime rain . . .

SŌSEKI

Out of the Heat and the Burden

What will may hap
  out in the world!—I, turning priest,
    go to my noonday nap!

SŌSEKI

Leaves

The winds that blow—
  ask them, which leaf of the tree
    will be next to go!

SŌSEKI

Me | wo | yande | hi | tomosanu | yo | ya | gogatsuame
Eyes | [acc.] | paining | lights | not-lit | night | : | May-rain

Ukiyo | ikani | bōzu | to narite | hirune | suru
World | whatever! | priest | becoming | noon-sleep | do

Kaze | ni | kike | izure | ga | saki-ni | chiru | ko-no-ha
Winds | to | ask | which | [subj.] | first-ly | falling | tree-leaf

The Parasol

Dear, your parasol,
  in all this blazing sunshine—
    is so very small!

SEIHŌ

City People

Townsfolk, it is plain—
  carrying red maple leaves
    in the homebound train.

MEISETSU

The Flower Wreath

Butterflies
  love and follow this flower wreath—
    that on the coffin lies.

MEISETSU

Retsujitsu | *ni* | *kimi-no* | *higasa-no* | *chiisasa* | *yo*
Blazing-sunshine | in | you [lady]'s | parasol's | smallness | !

Miyakobito | *ya* | *momiji* | *kazashite* | *modori-gisha*
City-people | *ya* | red-leaves | holding-up | returning-train

Students may be interested in the possibility that this haiku was suggested by a famous old *tanka* about court nobles holding up cherry blossoms: "*Inishie no/ omiyabito wa/ itoma ari ya/ sakura kazashite/ kyō mo kurashitsu.*"

Chōchō-no | *shitau* | *hara-wa* | *ya* | *kan-no* | *ue*
Butterflies' | lovingly-follow |
flower-wreath | *ya* | coffin's | top

The Good Neighbor

Night, and the moon!
My neighbor, playing on his flute—
out of tune!

KŌYŌ

Sounds

Insects one hears—
and one hears the talk of men—
with different ears.

WAFŪ

The Dragonfly

The dragonfly:
his face is very nearly
only eye!

CHISOKU

Yoru | tsuki | ni | mazui | fue | fuku | tonari | kana
Night | moon | in | poorly | flute | playing | neighbor | *kana*

Mushi | kiku-to | hanashi | wo | kiku-to | betsu-no | mimi
Insects | when-hear | conversation | [acc.] | when-hear | different | ears

Tombō-no | kao | wa | ō-kata | medama | kana
Dragonfly's | face | as-for | mostly | eyeball | *kana*

Constancy

Though it be broken—
  broken again—still it's there:
    the moon on the water.

CHOSHŪ

Kudakutemo | *kudakutemo* | *ari* | *mizu-no* | *tsuki*
Though-breaking | though-breaking | exists | water's | moon

Loneliness

No sky at all;
  no earth at all—and still
    the snowflakes fall. . . .

HASHIN

Ten | *mo* | *chi* | *mo* | *nashi* | *tada* | *yuki* | *no* | *furishikiri*
Sky | too | earth | too | are-not | only | snow | [sub.] |
falls-ceaselessly

APPENDIX

THE following list of *kireji* and other particles is given for the use of those who may wish to go back to the original Japanese as literally translated and transliterated for each poem; it is very cursory and does not attempt to be an exhaustive grammatical analysis. *Kireji* are particles with special uses in haiku and get their name, which means "cutting-words," from the fact that one of their functions is to indicate either a pause or a final stop. All particles are suffixes or "postpositions" in the sense that they affect only the words they follow. In reading haiku any pause must be made *after* the particles, not before them. The one exception is when *to* is used after quotations, etc., to indicate that "thus" one spoke or acted.

GA A particle with several uses. In older haiku, and those written in the "literary" language (*bungo*), usually equivalent to a possessive ('s). In the later colloquial it is used to mark the grammatical subject of a verb. Between phrases it may have the effect of "but."

KA A verbal question mark.

KANA A special *kireji* used to mark the end of a haiku. It has an undefinable emotional effect, sometimes like that of a soft sigh, more often that of a preceding "Ah!" or "Oh!" It usually follows a noun that the first part of the poem has described. As normal Japanese sentences end with a verb, *kana* may be considered as in a sense substituting for it.

KERI   A *kireji* marking either a pause or final stop. It was originally a verb suffix indicating a past tense, but has now no special meaning.

MO   A particle indicating that what it follows is added to something else. If that something has been mentioned *mo* is usually equivalent to "too" or "also"; if nothing has been mentioned, *mo* may be more nearly like "even." After verb forms it gives the effect of "even if," "even though."

MO . . . MO   When *mo* is used in parallel sequence its additive force is greatly intensified, and suggests also all other things (or actions) of the same kind.

NI   A postposition with many uses (at, in, to, by, for, etc.). These are usually indicated sufficiently in the literal translations. It is, however, important to realize that when *ni* is used after words indicating places, there is no action at that place.

NO   A particle indicating that one substantive in some way will characterize another. It may sometimes be indicated by a hyphen, or " 's" or simply positionally. E.g.: *asa-no-yuki* (morning's snow, morning snow, etc.). On the other hand, *yuki-no-asa* (snow-morning) is probably best translated as "snowy morning." The characterization is not always clear. Therefore, if one wishes to distinguish between a morning when snow is falling, against one where snow is simply there, one puts in the verb "to fall," so that *yuki-no-furu asa* is "a snow-falling morning," etc.

TO   Originally a reflexive "that," with several uses. Its most common use in haiku is to indicate "that" one said or did, or "thus" one spoke or acted. Its next most common usage is in tying nouns together, as in counting "that, and that, and that." Here it can be translated only by some paraphrase like "and" or "with." In any obvious series a *to* may be omitted. But it cannot be omitted if it is desired to emphasize that two or three or more things are on an absolute equality. E.g.: *Kyaku to teishu to shira-giku to* (host, guest, white chrysanthemum) by Ryōta (Buson's Contemporaries, p. 119). Occasionally, after certain verb forms, *to* will indicate "that happening, and then," and will have to be translated as "when" or "if" that happens.

WA   A particle which is usually followed by a noticeable pause. It is much like an English "as for" so-and-so, in that it not only marks what we are talking about, but also suggests a comparison with other things not mentioned.

WO   A postposition indicating that something is to be acted on, often, but not always, as the direct object of a verb. It can be likened to an accusative case ending.

YA   A *kireji* which has something of the effect of a preceding "Lo!" It divides a haiku into two parts and is usually followed by a description or comparison, sometimes by an illustration of the feeling evoked. There is always at least the suggestion of a kind of equation, so that the effect of *ya* is often best indicated by a colon. (The particle *ya* is not always a *kireji*. After certain verb forms, for example, it may indicate a rhetorical question. Such uses are indicated in the literal translations.)

YARA   A *kireji* indicating an emotional uncertainty, a sort of "I wonder!"

YO   A verbal exclamation mark.

ZO   A strong intensifier, either of a statement or a question. The combination *zo yo* has some of the effect of an interjection "Look!"

The importance of particles in haiku can be illustrated by an anonymous "country" haiku which has two forms, one using *ni,* the other *wo:* "*Kome arau mae ni* [or *wo*] *hotaru futatsu mitsu.*" Both could be translated as "In front of the washer of rice, fireflies, two or three." But when *ni* is used, there is no action; the fireflies are quiescent; there is a feeling of loneliness and sadness. When *wo* is used, the place is "acted on"; the fireflies are flitting around; there is a sense of expectancy—the girl's lover is coming—and a feeling of impending joy.

Kome | *arau* | *mae* | *ni* [*wo*] | *hotaru* | *futatsu-mitsu*
Rice | wash | front | at | fireflies | two-three

Those who do go back to the original Japanese must remember that the Japanese order of thought is almost the direct opposite of ours, due in large part to the fact that they have no relative pronouns, and that every strictly grammatical sentence must end with a verb. Thus one cannot say: "I saw the man who arrived here yesterday." One has to say "I (*wa*) yesterday here-at arrive-did man (*wo*) saw." (There is no "a" or "the.") Also, in my "literal" translations, although I have tried to give the nearest English equivalents, I have not always succeeded. There are practically no Japanese words that have one, and only one, English translation.